The Priestley Claim to Shelf Hall

Brenda Jackson

To Joan & Raymond
Best wishes Brenda Jackson

For Peter, Philip and Helen

First Published 2007
by
Beckside Publishers

ISBN 978-0-9557347-0-0

Printed by Lamberts Print & Design
2 Station Road, Settle, North Yorkshire, BD24 9AA

Contents

List of Figures

Foreword

The basis of this story has been known in my husband's family for many years. As an incomer to the family I was intrigued by this and eventually, after several years' research, I became as passionate about their claim to the Shelf Hall Estate as Rebecca and her syndicate. I felt I must tell the story if only to show their fight and determination for what they believed was truly theirs.

I must thank my mother-in-law and sister-in-law for recording hundreds of parish records. I am grateful to Cyril Metcalf's widow for allowing me to reproduce a copy of a photograph of Old Shelf Hall. Thanks go to Calderdale Library for allowing me to print the drawing of Shelf Hall by Arthur Cumfort also, to the Halifax Evening Courier for the copy of the photograph of Shelf Hall.

I give particular thanks to Carol Greenwood, Librarian in the Local Studies Department at Bradford Central Library for her help and encouragement, and Jennifer Gill, my friend and neighbour, for casting an expert eye on my work.

Finally, I thank my husband, Peter for correcting my spelling and grammar.

The Lean Years

Grace and Thomas

Grace and Tommy woke early. It was Christmas Day but they had neither Christmas presents to open nor special meal to eat. It was simply a day like any other. They had found it difficult to make ends meet since Tommy's father died. Grace Priestley married Thomas Henry Jackson on 28th July 1917. Tommy was born in 1920. Sixteen years later Thomas died. Poignant words on his memorial bookmark read:

> Farewell, dear husband,
> Father dear,
> From this sad life of toil
> and care,
> Let's hope to meet in
> Heaven above,
> And re-unite in God's own
> love

The death of the main breadwinner could plunge a family into poverty in the 1920s and 1930s in Bradford in the West Riding of Yorkshire. The General Strike and long periods of short time working were equally devastating. Fortunately, Grace had only one child to provide for. Larger families in such a situation could be destitute.

13, Crystal Terrace, Dudley Hill, Bradford was their home. It was a 'one up, one down' cottage at the end of a row of similar cottages. The row was probably named after the Crystal Palace. The 'one up' was reached by steep stone steps. The room, shared by Grace and Tommy, contained a double bed, a broken chest of drawers and a string suspended between two nails in the wall on which Tommy hung his trousers and jacket. There was no rug on the floor, just the bare, untreated boards. The gas mantle on the wall was damaged and unsafe to use so they lit the room with candles.

The 'one down' was used as kitchen, parlour, washroom and bathroom. The room focussed on the Yorkshire Range, a combination of room heater, oven and cooker, constructed from cast iron, pans being heated over the open fire. The range was the only facility for cooking and heating water in most working class households. It was fuelled by coal, which was delivered in sacks by horse and cart, the sacks being emptied down a chute straight into the cellar. It was Tommy's job to get the coal from the cellar and make the fire. When times were hard and they could not afford a coal delivery, they burnt any pieces of wood they could find. During the days and weeks of strikes and short time working friends and neighbours would compete for any combustible material.

To one side of the range was a large cupboard in which Grace stored food, crockery, pots and pans. To the other side of the range in the corner was the cellar head giving access to the cellar steps. This small area contained a shallow stone sink, cold water tap and gas ring. The gas ring was connected to the main gas supply by a rubber tube, which was perished and had a slight leak. The smell of gas and household odours lingered throughout the house.

Grace had a wooden rocking chair, two dining chairs and a deal table. The table was the centre of most activities in every household. Baking, washing, preparing food and eating were all done at the table. It was scrubbed clean daily and proudly covered with a thick tablecloth on high days and holidays. Apart from a small mahogany clock that hung on the wall, the sideboard was the only undamaged piece of furniture in the house. The lavatories were outside, reached by a rough track and up a flight of steps that led into a field. Two households shared each lavatory. Every home had a chamber pot under the bed to use during the night, rather than venturing out in the cold and dark. Adjacent to number thirteen was a pigsty. These extremely

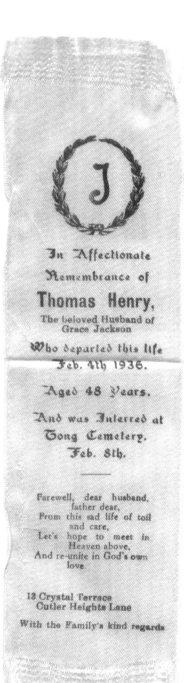

Figure 1.
Thomas Henry
Jackson's
Memorial,
printed on silk
ribbon.

In Affectionate
Remembrance of

Thomas Henry,
The beloved Husband of
Grace Jackson

Who departed this life
Feb. 4th 1936.

Aged 48 Years.

And was Interred at
Bong Cemetery.
Feb. 8th.

Farewell, dear husband,
father dear,
From this sad life of toil
and care,
Let's hope to meet in
Heaven above,
And re-unite in God's own
love.

13 Crystal Terrace
Cutler Heights Lane

With the Family's kind regards

poor living conditions were not untypical of many working class homes.

Friday night was bath night. Grace would build up the fire in the range to boil water in readiness for the tin bath, which was placed in front of the fire. The fire kept the bathwater warm, so although the water in larger households would be dirty for the last to bathe, at least it would not be cold.

It had been usual for many years for the family to visit Grace's sister Eliza and her husband Lawson Hudson on Christmas Day. The visit was still continued even after the death of Eliza and Thomas Henry. Tommy looked forward to the outing on Christmas Day. It was a frosty day. They knew this because frost had formed on the inside of the windows, the bedroom being almost as cold inside as out. They set off walking quickly to keep warm. Few people were out on the streets those they saw were greeted by a cheery 'Merry Christmas'. Tommy noticed that Grace began walking more slowly. 'Come on Mum, keep up' he said. She did not answer but continued to slow her pace. Having gained a few yards, he turned round and walked back towards her, noticing she had tears in her eyes. He was shocked and speechless. He had rarely seen her cry. Seconds went by before he moved, then he quickly put his arm around her and said, 'What's wrong, Mum? Why are you crying?' As she very quickly turned round she replied,

'We're going home.' Tommy was confused. He ran to catch up with her, saying,

'What's wrong, what's wrong?' When he caught up he noticed that the tears had gone. Neither spoke again on the short walk back home.

Tommy helped her off with her coat and hung it with his behind the door. Grace put coal on the fire and sat down in her rocking chair. She started to rock whilst tapping her foot on the stone flagged floor. The tapping normally annoyed Tommy, but somehow this time it comforted him, as an indication that normality had returned. He was unsure whether to ask her again what was wrong. Grace sensed his uncertainty and said, 'I'm not going to let your uncle Lawson think we need to go there on Christmas Day because we need his charity.'

'But I don't think uncle Lawson would ever think that, Mum' Tommy replied.

'Nay, Tommy, we can feed ourselves. My family has not always been poor', she said, 'Remember you are a Priestley as much as a Jackson.'

'But I'm called Jackson, who were the Priestleys?' Tommy asked.

'The Priestleys were......

Figure 2. Number 13 Crystal Terrace where Thomas, Grace and Tommy lived. Today, a comfortable home with a bathroom.

The Origins of the Priestley Name

As it became necessary for individuals to require a surname these surnames developed from one of four basic roots, a patronymic relationship, a nickname, place of birth or a person's occupation. In the case of the name Priestley, it is likely that this was the latter. The likelihood of this was that 'the man who dwelt by the priest's wood' and assisted the priest in 'clearing the woodland' The man took on the name 'Priest' and 'Leah' meaning 'wood clearer' eventually added the suffix 'Leah' or 'Ley' to the word Priest, becoming Priestley.

The origin of the name Priestley and its variant spelling has its roots firmly established in the West Riding of Yorkshire. As there is a significant number of the surname recorded in parish

Figure 3. A Priestley Coat of Arms above a window at 'White Windows', a house at Sowerby Bridge.
(By kind permission of the "Leonard Cheshire" organisation).

records, wills and other documents, in the West Riding, it must be considered to be a truly regional surname. The Priestleys are recorded as being landowners in and round Soyland near Halifax since William the Conqueror. Memoirs concerning the Priestleys of Goodgreave, Soyland were written by Jonathan Priestley in 1696. He gives an excellent account of the Priestley pedigree and details of the houses occupied by Priestleys. White Windows in Sowerby Bridge was built by John Priestley in 1680 and occupied by Priestleys until 1840. Apart from a plaster cast Priestley coat of arms in the stairway at Whitewindows, an etching of the name 'John Priestley' is there in evidence on one of the windowpanes. Bentley Royd at Sowerby, Priestley Green at Hipperholme, Westercroft and Winteredge near Shelf were all in Priestley possession. Johannes Priestley occupied the Manor of Shelf Hall at the time of the Dissolution of the Monasteries.

The Priestleys dominated areas of Halifax, Elland, Soyland, Sowerby and Greetland, eventually moving northwards into Bradford. At the onset of the industrial revolution they, like so many families, moved in great numbers into the southern part of the town, where work was in abundance. Parts of Wibsey, Low Moor and Great Horton became Priestley enclaves. This cohesion of Priestley families took on a 'clan-like' form, well into the twentieth century.

The Prosperous Years

James Priestley (The Will)

James was a successful clothier and Yeoman farmer in Shelf near Bradford. He had inherited the family home, the Manor of Shelf, known as Shelf Hall Farm, from his father, also called James. On 2nd December 1706 he married a widow, Sarah Surridge at St John the Baptist church, Halifax. It was with Sarah that James had his children.

After Sarah's death, James married Mary Dixon, a widow from Oldfield near Keighley in the West Riding. They were married in Halifax in 1732. James had a further fifteen years marriage with Mary until his death in 1747.

Primogeniture, the custom of leaving land and property to the firstborn son had been practise in England for centuries. However, this custom changed and partible inheritance whereby the division of property among all or some of the children of a family, rather than leaving everything to the eldest son, became popular. It was this division that James Priestley decided upon when he made his will on 25th April 1747. He was not to know that 146 years later his will would be part of a law suit. His descendents John, Rebecca, Abraham, Albert and Elizabeth were the leading players in the case. John was to become the heir-at-law to the estate. Rebecca, his aunt, was a member of his immediate family, whilst Abraham and Elizabeth belonged to another branch of the family and Albert Priestley belonged to a third branch. These three branches of the family came together to form the 'Priestley Litigation'.

The will of James Priestley of Shelf

April 25th 1747

In the name of God, Amen! The twenty-fifth day of April in the year of our Lord one thousand seven hundred and forty seven, I, James Priestley, of Shelf in the County of York, yeoman, being of sound and disposing mind and memory, thanks be to God! do make and ordain this my last will and testament in manner following:-

I give and devise to my eldest son James Priestley and his heirs, the messuage where I now dwell with all the buildings, outhouses, gardens, appurtenances and closes and parcels of ground therewith occupied, and all the every tenements and hereditaments in Shelf aforesaid, in whose tenures or occupations soever the same or be for ever, and he to enter to the same immediately after my decease, chargeable nevertheless with the sum of ten pounds of lawful money of Great Britain to be paid to George Priestley, alias Holroyd, when he shall come to the age of twenty-one years, and I will that in case default shall be made in payment of the said sum of ten pounds or any part thereof within the time limited before for the payment thereof. That it shall and may be lawful for the said George Priestley, alias Holroyd, his executors, administrators or assignees into and upon all and every the said tenements and premises or any part or parts thereof to enter, and the rents, issues, and profits thereof to receive and take to his and their own use and uses till there out he and they shall of the said sum of ten pounds and every part thereof, and all damages and costs and charges occasioned or to be sustained by non-payment or recovery thereof, be fully satisfied and paid.

To my third son, Jonathan, and to his heirs lawfully begotten, I give and devise my messuage called Spring Hall, with the buildings, outhouses and gardens, and all appurtenances and closes and parcels of ground therewith occupied, and all and every the tenements and hereditaments in Shelf aforesaid, which I purchased of George Moore, in whose tenures and occupations soever the same are to be, and all my houses and barns, and all other appurtenances thereto belonging being now in the occupation of William Holmes or his assignees, situate in

Shelf aforesaid, and he or they to enter thereto immediately after my decease. And for default of such heirs as before mentioned all the said messuages, with all the appurtenances thereto belonging aforesaid. My mind further is and I hereby give and devise unto my two sons James Priestley and Joseph Priestley to each of their heirs for ever equally to be divided among them all and every tenement and premises hereinbefore devised to my said son Jonathan and his heirs.

To my dear wife I give one shilling and no more, she being entitled to a dower of five pounds twelve shillings and sixpence in the year during her life out of an estate called Oldfield, situate and being in the parish of Keighley and county aforesaid. And all the residue of my personal estate after payment of my just debts, funeral expenses and legacies. I give and bequeath unto my three sons James, Joseph and Jonathan equally to be divided amongst them, and I do constitute and appoint my two sons, Joseph and Jonathan, sole executors of this, my last will and testament, and my will further is that if my son James Priestley shall claim any part of my real estate other than what is herein to him respectfully devised, or shall demand against my executors any part of my personal estate and commence any suit or suits in any court of law or equity, or in any ecclesiastical court for recovery of any part of my real estate other than what is to him herein devised, or for the recovery against my executors any part of my personal estate than the devises therein contained for the benefit of him so commencing suit shall thenceforth cease and be void; and then I give and devise to my other two sons, Joseph and Jonathan, and to their heirs and assignees, equally to be divided amongst them all and every the tenements and premises hereinbefore devised to my said son James so commencing suit touching the premises and revoking all other wills by me heretofore made. I publish and declare this

to be my last will and testament the day and year first above written.
JAMES PRIESTLEY

An inventory of all the goods cattle chattels creditors and debts of James Priestley late of Shelf in the Parish of Halifax within the Diocese of York Clothier Deceased as they was viewed valued and prized the Twenty Sixth Day of May An Dom: 1747 by us whose names are Subscribed

First of all Purses and Apparel	1..0..0
House Body One Range one Poker one Cole rake and Tongs	0..4..0
Four Pots and three Pans	0..6..0
One Clock and Case	1..0..0
Certain Brass and Pewter	0.15..0
One Long Settle one Chest three Chairs and 2 Stools	0..5..0
One Bread Creel	0..1..0
Parlour One Bed and Bedding	1..5..0
One Cupboard and 2 Chairs	0..8..0
First Chamber Two Chairs and Table and Form	0..5..0
One S???ke	0..1..0
Second Chamber Two Chests	0..5..0
One Load of Meal	0.15..0
Milkhouse One Churn 2 Barrels 6 Bowls and Some Pots	0..4..0
Houselement	0..1..6
Barn Horse Gears and one Harrow	0..7..0
One Spade and Shovel and Fork	0..1..6
Houselement	0..7..6
Three Cows	5.10..0
One Horse	2..2..0
	in all 14..18..6

Jonathan Benn
William Greenwood
Richard Fawcet
Joseph Woodhead

Figure 4. Old Shelf Hall in 1923.

James Priestley (Son)

Throughout the centuries it had been customary to name sons after their father and grandfather, the Priestleys being no exception to this. James and Joseph are names, which appear in most Priestley families throughout the centuries. Like his father, James also married twice and had two families. One of his sons named Joseph settled in Bishop Auckland in County Durham. Joseph and his wife Hannah (nee Clement) had a large family, some of them settling in the North East of England and others in Addingham in the West Riding of Yorkshire.

The Priestleys chose the North East wisely, benefiting greatly from the building of the Stockton and Darlington Railway in 1825, guaranteeing work for many. Middlesbrough mushroomed in size, population and industry between 1801 and 1841. It was here that this Priestley branch settled.

Addingham had one of the first worsted spinning mills in 1800, some thirteen years before Bradford. Some of Joseph and Hannah's family worked in the mill. Both branches of the family kept in touch and later in the century, became hosts to Priestleys from Bradford. Other descendents of James, Joseph and Jonathan remained in Halifax and Bradford but none forgot about Shelf Hall and land and property willed by James.

The Illegitimate's Inheritance

George Priestley

George was born to Rose Holroyd, spinster of Shelf, illegitimate child of George Priestley labourer of Shelf, his baptism being recorded in St John the Baptist church, Halifax on 19th August 1733. George was the grandson of James Priestley and the son of James' son, George. James had stipulated in his will that George was to be given £10.0.0 at his coming of age of 21 years. If he were not given this he was to 'recover the said amount from any rents, issues or profits from the owner of Shelf Hall'.

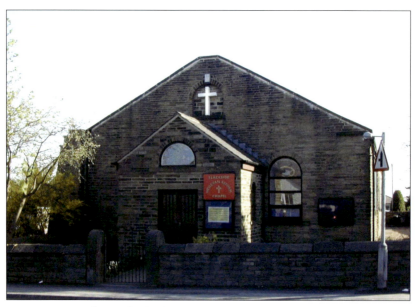

Figure 5. Wibsey Slackside Chapel where Benny played the organ.

George and his descendents settled in Horton Township in Bradford. Fathers, grandfathers, sons and daughters and all manner of in-laws lived cheek by jowl on Beldon Hill and Pickles Hill in Horton. The Priestley clan was firmly rooted in the area throughout the nineteenth and twentieth centuries.

Initially most were handloom weavers, but as the decades wore on and the mechanisation of the textile industry snowballed, many Priestleys descended the hills to work in the town. Other Priestleys left their looms in the hope of earning more money in the mines that had developed on the hillsides of Wibsey and Horton.

In 1841, Benjamin Priestley, a descendant of George's lived on Beldon Hill with his large family. He too was a weaver and still worked as a labourer at the age of 72 in 1881. However, Benny was a keen gardener and well known for growing dahlias and pansies. He and his family attended Wibsey Slackside Chapel where Benny played the organ. Benny lived in part of an old farmhouse where he had a trichord piano on which he played 'classical and sacred music'. But he also had a carved oak bed at least three hundred years old. George Priestley inherited this bed in part payment of his ten pounds inheritance from James Priestley. On the inventory of the goods, cattle and chattles of James Priestley's will is a bed and bedding to the value of one pound five shillings. Did George receive the remaining eight pounds fifteen shillings?

Poverty, Child Labour and the Workhouse

James and Nancy (Nanny)

The nation was celebrating Nelson's victory at Trafalgar in 1805 when James Priestley met Nancy (Nanny) Clayton. On 24th August 1806 James the weaver and Nanny the spinster were married at St. John the Baptist Church in Halifax. They were both from Ovenden, Halifax in the West Riding.

Shortly after their marriage they moved to the township of Bowling in Bradford. Bradford at this time was at the cusp of becoming the worsted capital of the world. James and his family were participants in the mechanisation of this product. From being a member of the 'putting out system' of producing a piece of cloth in his home, James became a slave to a machine in one of the many mills.

From the hillside of Bowling, James could look down into the town of Bradford and see the forest of mill chimneys densely filling the valley until the smoke obliterated his view. The young German Georg Weerth visited Bradford in the 1840s and he compared his entrance into the town with a descent into hell, summing up the town with these words:

> '...that you had been lodged in no other place than with the Devil incarnate....if anyone wants to feel how a poor sinner is perhaps tormented in Purgatory, let him travel to Bradford'

The population in Bradford in 1801 was 13,264 but by 1851 this was 103,778. The rural communities had decanted into towns like Bradford where work was plentiful, but living conditions were nothing better than squalid. It was with this backdrop that James and Nanny raised their family. Son James was born in 1809 and Martha was baptised on 19th June 1815 the day after Wellington defeated Napoleon at Waterloo. James often told his children about James Priestley's will and how he and they would, one day inherit a great deal of land and property.

James and Martha grew up in a town that was to change dramatically, but their children were to grow up in a town that was to change out of all recognition.

James and Elizabeth

James and Martha grew up during Bradford's industrial change. In October 1828 James married Elizabeth Wardman. Neither could sign their name in the marriage register at St. Peters church in Bradford. Elizabeth had more than ten children, but not all survived beyond infancy. This was quite common in the nineteenth century because of the high incidence of disease and poor living conditions. Bradford was seriously polluted by smoke and refuse. There was neither sewage system nor fresh water,

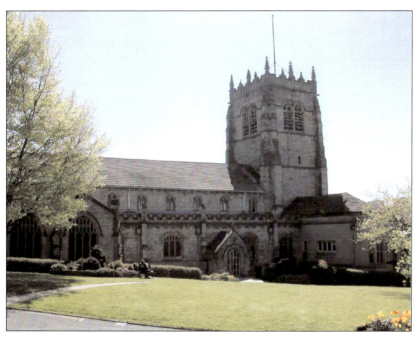

Figure 6. St Peter's Parish Church Bradford (Now Bradford Cathedral).

food was adulterated and poor housing and overcrowding caused epidemics. The average age of death in the town was twenty years and three months.

Bradford's shame, at the time, came from its factories' need for a massive workforce and most of these were women and children. Children as young as eight years old worked in the factories for twelve to thirteen hours a day. The 'factory children' were nothing better than slaves. The slave trade had been abolished in 1807, but slavery was thriving in the West Riding of Yorkshire in the 1820s and 30s.

Children had worked at home and on the land, with their parents and siblings, but this work depended upon the weather conditions. On fine days they would be out in the fields with the benefit of the sunshine and fresh air. The factory system of working imposed a strict discipline and order on them, usually behind closed doors. Children would go to work and return home in the winter darkness. The machinery they operated was dangerous, accidents being common and often fatal. Many children suffered deformities and stunted growth due to the cramped working conditions.

Very many children were victims of physical abuse at the hands of the overlookers at the mill. Children were beaten with a strap, rope or a hand by these men, simply for being late for work, talking or falling asleep at their machine. Many of the overlookers were tyrants. James Priestley was an overlooker and his children factory children. As an overlooker James would have earned a little more than the average mill operative, yet he had lodgers living with him and his family to assist in paying the rent. Bradford had become a pulsating town in 1840 with an insatiable appetite for workers who needed somewhere to live near their place of work. Those with a roof over their heads offered accommodation to incomers, many having travelled across the Irish Sea or from the Highlands of Scotland, perhaps as a result of the Scottish Highland clearances, another inhumanity that was taking place at the time.

In 1841 James and Elizabeth lived in Peel Street in the Barkerend area of the parish. Their children Joseph, Rebecca, Elizabeth-Ann and grandmother Nanny also lived with them. Six years later Nanny went to live with her daughter Martha, at Slack, Wibsey where she died aged seventy-one. In 1851 the family moved to Priestley Street, a street behind the Parish church, where James and Elizabeth were married. Priestley Street and Captain Street were named after Captain John Priestley. John held a commission in the 32nd Regiment of Foot, in the early 1800s, as a result of this he was known as Captain Priestley.

John's father, Joseph Priestley was the superintendent of the Leeds and Liverpool Canal and lived at Stott Hill Hall, one of the principal homesteads in Bradford's early history. Joseph Priestley's father was called James Priestley of Shelf. It is very likely that Joseph was the son, named in the will of 1747. Whilst living at Priestley Street John (Jack), James and Benjamin (Jem) and another Elizabeth was born to James and Elizabeth. In 1857, aged forty-eight, James died. Elizabeth did not fare well after James's death; her fate was to become a charwoman. Had she not had support from her family, she may have ended up in the workhouse.

Joseph

Joseph was born as James and Elizabeth's first son during the reign of William IV. He was baptised on the 26th February 1834, the year of the fire at the Palace of Westminster. Joseph was to witness some of the most profound events in Bradford's history in his forty-eight years of life.

The living and working conditions in Bradford, during his early life were appalling. Employment was unpredictable for many men. It was women and children who were the fodder for the machines, in the factories. Mechanization was misery for all but the millmasters. These conditions generated a great deal of unrest, in the town. As a consequence, the Chartist Movement took hold in the 1840's. Joseph probably saw the men marching in the streets in support of the movement.

Disease and premature death were common. Pollution was a major cause of epidemic and ill health in the overcrowded slums in the town. The cholera outbreak in 1849 killed four hundred and twenty six people, young and old. Perhaps he knew some of those who died. Many were buried at Greenhill Wesleyan Chapel, not far from his own home. Joseph and his brothers and sisters became child workers in a worsted mill. The land and property that grandfather James said they would inherit seemed an impossible dream. But Joseph and his brothers, Jem and Jack were determined to state their claim to the land at Shelf in any way they could.

There was a great deal of competition for jobs during the 1840s and 50s, due to the influx of immigrants into Bradford. These migrants came from all parts of the British Isles and a small, but influential, commercial group came from Germany. However, it was the poverty stricken Irish immigrants from the rural, peasant regions of the West of Ireland who settled in Bradford in large numbers. They first started to arrive in the town in the 1820's. But, there was a build up of migrants during 1835-45 when firstly poverty and then the potato blight 'phytophthora infestans' caused the 'Great Famine' in Ireland. Migration or annihilation were their only options.

It was whilst Joseph was working in the mill that he met Catherine McLaughlin. Catherine came to Bradford from Killarney, Co Kerry in the 1840's. She left behind a country affected by famine and its consequences. She and her family would have travelled from Killarney to Dublin and then by boat to England, through Liverpool's revolving door. She must have looked back at the beautiful lakes around Killarney with a little regret. Catherine was not to know her fate in the West Riding of Yorkshire. Both twenty-four years old, Catherine and Joseph were married on the 25th May 1857. Joseph's father, James died six months later.

The union of a protestant and a catholic was not common at

the time in Bradford and was not without its difficulties. There was much hostility towards the Irish in the town. Their language, customs, culture and religion were little tolerated by the host community. They were not made welcome. As a result of these hostilities and their low wages they were obliged to settle in poor, rundown areas of the parish. These areas became known as the 'Irish Quarters' where they had to eke out some kind of an existence. Catherine and Joseph settled in one of the most squalid of all quarters, the Goit Side. It was at Green Aire Place on 13th April 1858 that Mary-Ann Priestley was born.

The density of the population in Goit Side created serious over crowding. Most families had lodgers and boarders, which frequently resulted in the need to share a bed, often there were two or three people sharing a bed at one time. It was only at the time of a woman's confinement that she had sole occupancy of a bed. Catherine and Joseph moved to 64 West End Street, Goit Side, in 1860. It was here that twins Emma and Hannah were born on the 29th July 1860. By the end of the year Catherine and the children were admitted to the union workhouse as paupers. At this time, Joseph was living and working in Todmorden, a busy little Yorkshire town near the Lancashire boarder.

Rules, regulations and bell ringing governed life in the workhouse. Paupers had to stick to the rules and respond to the bell ringing, or they were punished. Everyone had a job to do to earn a place in the workhouse. Catherine would have worked in either the kitchen or laundry, with the other women. If the paupers were ill, the union workhouse doctor saw them and their children were vaccinated against some diseases. Had they been living in the town they may not have been able to afford such treatment. There were some treats for the children in the workhouse. Pablo's circus came to Bradford in April 1861 and the board of guardians gave the paupers permission to attend the circus providing the workhouse were not charged for this!

Paupers were coming in and out of workhouse care. They would tell the inmates about events happening outside. Whilst

Catherine was in the workhouse the American Civil War broke out causing a blockade of cotton from the southern parts of North America. This 'Cotton Famine' brought hardship to the mill workers in both Lancashire and Yorkshire. If cotton was not being imported, mill workers were 'laid off.' Perhaps Joseph suffered from being laid off in his job in Todmorden, as a result of the blockade. In 1864 Joseph returned to Bradford and at the same time, Catherine and the children left the workhouse.

In 1864 Joseph and his family were living at Pit Lane in the Barkerend area of the parish. It was whilst here, in June 1865, that John Edwin was born. The family moved to 4 Farrar Square, Pit Lane, where Charles was born in 1868. In 1869 Mary Ann was eleven, the twins Emma and Hannah were nine, John was four and Charles was one year old. In July Catherine complained of

Figure 7. The Bradford workhouse where Catherine lived with her three children. Now part of St. Luke's NHS Hospital.

pains in her 'insides'. She was seen by several doctors, all of whom treated her, but with little effect. She began to say strange things: 'she was going out of her mind', and that 'her husband and children would be lost'. She refused food and would not wash herself, because 'she feared she was going to be drowned'. Catherine did not attempt nor even speak of suicide.

On the 11th November 1869 Catherine was at home at Farrar Square in an anxious and distressed state. She was interviewed by Dr Anchia Rabagliati and told him that a 'policeman would remove her children, she knew not where but he would do them some injury'. She also said that she would 'lose her soul'. Catherine was clearly depressed. So many desperate things had happened to her since her childhood in Ireland. Perhaps the period of separation from Joseph and her time in the workhouse had seriously affected her. She may have been affected by Charles's birth and her marriage to a protestant. The priest and her family may have suggested that she could lose her soul because she had married out of her religion. All of these events were too much for Catherine. She was admitted to Wakefield Lunatic Asylum on the 11th November 1869, where she remained until her death on the 22nd December 1874. After her admission to the asylum it is unlikely that she ever saw her children again.

Joseph and Ann

After Catherine was admitted to the asylum, Joseph and the children went to live with his mother Elizabeth, brother John and sister Elizabeth at North Wing, one of the many streets behind the parish church. In 1871 Mary Ann and the twins Emma and Hannah worked as stuff piecers in the local mill. Their job was to tie the broken threads on the spinning machines. Young girls were small and nimble their tiny fingers were ideal for tying the broken threads. They worked in smelly, dirty and dangerous conditions, for long hours. They had not only lost their mother, but also their childhood. The poet Elizabeth Barrett Browning, wrote in the 1840's 'The Cry of the Children':

The young lambs are bleating in the meadows,
   The young birds are chirping in the nest,
The young fawns are playing with the shadows,
   The young flowers are blowing towards the west-
But the young, young children, O my brothers,
   They are weeping bitterly!
They are weeping in the playtime of the others,
   In the country of the free

Joseph was informed of Catherine's death in 1874 a few days before Ann Atlay informed the registrar in Bradford, of her husband's death. Joseph met Ann shortly after their respective losses. They were married on the 18th May 1875. Ann (nee Sunter) was born in the lead-mining area of Brownberry, Low Row on the fringe of Melbeck Moor in the North Riding of Yorkshire. In 1835 Ann married Edward Fawcett and they moved to Bradford where they had their family. Edward died suddenly leaving Ann to raise their children. Ann married Richard Atlay, a wood carver from Sheriff Hutton near York, in 1859. Richard had his own wood carving business in the town but he too died, leaving Ann a widow once again.

Joseph and Ann lived at Wakefield Road in Bradford in 1881. Mary Ann, Hannah and her husband and child, John and Charles also lived there. Joseph worked at the local mill where he was an engine tenter, but he was an ill man. He was forty-five years old and he had serious heart and lung disease, probably due to hard work and poor living conditions. The town was forested by very many mills, their chimney's filling the air with black smoke. The soot in the smoke stained the buildings black and also coated the lungs of many Bradfordians. These poor victims had what was later known as 'the Bradford lung'. Joseph was one of those many victims.

In 1881 Joseph was admitted to the North Bierley Union Workhouse, where he died on the 11th November. Mary Ann, his daughter, the little girl at three years old, had also spent some of her life in the workhouse, registered his death. Ann Priestley, his wife, died five years later.

Rebecca

As James and Elizabeth's eldest daughter, Rebecca, often called 'Becca, was born on the 9th March 1837 the year Victoria ascended the throne. Joseph was four years older than she. When she was born, the family lived at Peel Street in Bradford township. Rebecca grew up in the 'hungry 40's' when the population of the town escalated. There was overcrowding, poor housing and low wages. The majority of the population, in the town, lived on the edge of poverty. The town was seen as lawless. Violence, drunkenness and crime were rife. But it was children like Rebecca who were most vulnerable, from the risk of accidents and contagious disease. Tuberculosis, measles, scarlet fever and cholera were common and thrived in squalid, slum conditions. Elizabeth Ann, Rebecca's sister was always a sickly child and died before reaching adulthood. When James and Elizabeth had their next daughter they named her Elizabeth in anticipation of the death of Elizabeth Ann. It was not uncommon in the nineteenth century to name another child after one that had died.

Like so many working class children at this time, Rebecca became a mill child. By the age of fourteen Rebecca was a power loom weaver, she had no education, and could not sign her name in the church register, when she married Joshua Brown in 1860. She and Joshua lived in Bradford but do not appear to have had any children. This must have been a great disappointment to Rebecca. Joshua and Rebecca may have experienced some insult and ridicule from family and friends because of their inability to produce children, which was expected in the Victorian era. Infertility was uncommon and misunderstood and seen as unnatural.

The public house played an important part in the life of many working class men during Joshua's lifetime. There was a plethora of dram shops, beer shops and public houses in Bradford when

Joshua was a young man. However, there were those who saw the horror caused by the 'demon drink' and wanted to do something about it. Henry Forbes, a Bradford businessman held these views and helped set up the Bradford Temperance Society in 1830. Men were encouraged to sign 'the pledge' vowing to drink no intoxicants except for medicinal or sacramental purposes. Church attendance, clubs, theatre and meetings were encouraged as an alternative to drinking alcohol. However, such recreation was beyond the purse and understanding of the average working man. Perhaps Joshua Brown was such a man.

On the 2nd August 1878, whilst at his work Joshua had an accident. The inquest relating to Joshua was reported in the 'Bradford Chronicle'.

FATAL ACCIDENT IN BRADFORD

An inquest was held at the Town Hall, this morning, by Mr J G Hutchinson, borough coroner, touching the death of Joshua Brown, wool extractor, of 172, Barkerend Road – Rebecca Brown, wife of the deceased, stated that he was 42 years of age, and was employed by Mr Henry Lee, North Wing. On the 2nd August, she went to him at his work, and requested him to go home and have some tea, as he was in a bad state of health. The deceased was putting a belt on the engine, after which he put some resin on the belt to give it a 'bite'. Whilst doing this he struck his head against a portion of the engine when in motion, and he fell forward on to it. He was immediately taken out, and conveyed to the Infirmary, where he died, last Monday evening. He had been a heavy drinker, and for a few weeks before the accident he had not been well. Mr William Lake Roberts, house surgeon at the Infirmary proved that the deceased's head was injured, and several bones were broken. A few days before his death he was attacked with lockjaw, and death resulted in consequence – The jury returned a verdict of 'Accidental Death'.

The report implies that Joshua may have sustained the accident because he was a 'heavy drinker' thereby exempting Mr Henry Lee from any liability. Accidents and fatalities, to employees were common in mills like Mr Lee's. Safety guards and safety equipment were rarely fitted to machinery. If employers were able to blame an accident on the employee it would save them a great deal of money in compensation. In Joshua's case Mr Lee must have been pleased to hear that Joshua was a 'heavy drinker'.

Rebecca, now a widow, had no children but many nieces and nephews. She would often tell them the family story of Shelf Hall and James Priestley. Joseph's eldest son John liked to hear the story and wondered how different his life would be if he were to own Shelf Hall.

Rebecca and William

Rebecca Brown married William Crellin on 3rd October 1880 at Calverley Church near Bradford. William was born on the Isle of Man in 1843. He and his ten brothers and sisters lived at Moaneemolloch at Kirk Michael, where his father had a dye works, house and small plot of land. Many people left the island for work in the towns of Lancashire and Yorkshire during the nineteenth century. Therefore, there was little need for the Crellin's business. As a consequence, William's father became bankrupt and the house and dye works were sold. William left the island and settled in Bradford where his skills in the dyeing trade were in demand.

William met Rebecca at the mill where they both worked. They lived in Bradford during their early years of marriage but later moved to Leeds in the West Riding. They lived at Clifford Street in Kirkstall with their lodger, William Foster, known as 'Willie'. Willie, a grocer's assistant, heard about a grocer's shop for rent in Cavendish Street, Kirkstall and persuaded Rebecca to leave her work in the mill and become a shopkeeper. Rebecca, William and Willie moved in. It was in this little shop that Rebecca and her family often met to discuss their family's lost inheritance.

Figure 8. The present day site of William Crellin's home and dyehouse, Moaneemolloch.

Hard Labour, Childbirth and Tragedy

Ely

Ely Priestley and Maria Ellis married on 17th August 1806 one week before James Priestley married Nancy (Nanny) Clayton, at St. John the Baptist church in Halifax. Ely and James had grown up together and both knew the family story of Shelf Hall. James and Nanny moved to Bradford shortly after their marriage, whilst Ely and Maria settled in Halifax. Ely was a navigator or 'navvy' and worked on constructing the canal in and around Halifax. This work was hard and dangerous, as too was childbirth. Maria had given birth to eleven children, but died giving birth to Ellen. Whilst the people of Halifax were celebrating the opening of the Calder and Hebble Canal in 1828, Ely was mourning the death of Maria. He was left to rear new baby Ellen, three-year-old Maria, and six year old Jeremiah with help from Thomas, his second son. Maternal deaths were not uncommon and husbands could be left with many children to care for. The workhouse was the only help available to families like Ely's. Fortunately, Ely met Elizabeth Gaukroger and on 5th November 1829 they were

Figure 10. The Lock-Keeper's Cottage where Ely lived with Elizabeth.

38

married. The family settled in Elland, a few miles East of Halifax. Ely continued working on the canals and his sons got work in the quarries. Ely became a Lock Keeper at Long Lee, Elland. He lived in the Lock Keepers house were he was a popular character on the canal. He died in his sixty eighth year of life. Thomas, his son was with him when he died.

Thomas

As Ely and Maria's second son, Thomas Priestley was baptised on 13th October 1811 at St. John the Baptist church, Halifax. He was born during the Luddite activities that started in Nottingham and later spread to Huddersfield and Halifax. The Luddites set up one of their secret societies in Halifax and held some of their meetings at St. Crispin Inn, next to the church where Thomas was baptised. Thomas and his brother John worked together as delvers, at a time when the industry was booming. During the 1850-60's there was a great demand for stone, for building purposes, the larger towns of Yorkshire and Lancashire having extensive building programmes. There was a need for houses, mills and civic buildings. The prosperous wool towns wanted to display their prosperity by building public buildings of distinction. There was rivalry between Leeds and Bradford as to which had the grandest town hall, at the time. Halifax built a splendid town hall in 1863, designed by the acclaimed Sir Charles Barry.

In 1835 Thomas married Elizabeth Broadbent, in Elland near Halifax. They lived in the Southowram parish of the town, where several of their children were born. Some of Thomas's children were named after his grandparents, but in 1845 Albert was born. He was probably named after Prince Albert, Queen Victoria's husband. When Albert was twenty years old he married Harriet Parker. At this time he worked on the railway in Halifax. Halifax had a network of old packhorse routes, paths and lanes, like pedestrian motorways and used by most people unless they were wealthy enough to have a horse. The railways replaced these routes with a mode of transport that helped shrink the country. The railways further facilitated Albert's travel to Bradford and Leeds to visit his Priestley relatives.

Maria

Maria Priestley, named after her mother, was baptised on 13th February 1825 at St John the Baptist church in Halifax. Within three years of her baptism, her mother died giving birth to her sister Ellen. Many young children in the Victorian era lost one or both parents to disease or accidents. Women often died in childbirth because of their frequent pregnancies, increased age, poor health and the risk of infection. Whole families were left grieving and no one to care for them. The fortunate ones, like Maria, had a stepmother. Like so many girls in industrial towns like Halifax, Maria went to work in a mill. In 1846 she married George Cooper and lived in Morley in the West Riding where they had their family. George and their sons Ely and Benjamin worked in the coalmines. Coal was the life-blood of industry, trade and transport at this time. However, it was a very dangerous occupation. Working conditions were hazardous, damp and dark despite the introduction of the 'Davy' lamp.

By the early part of Victoria's reign the country was criss-crossed by the railway network, which revolutionised industry and people's lives. The Priestley families of Halifax, Bradford, Leeds and Middlesbrough visited each other thanks to the fuel of coal and the power of steam.

Figure 12. St. John the Baptist Church Halifax, where many Priestley baptism, marriage and funeral services were held.

Before Thomas and Grace. The Edge of Poverty

William and Elizabeth (Betty)

William Priestley and Elizabeth Shore were married at St. John the Baptist church in Halifax on 8th July 1810. Ely and Maria were married there in 1806 as were James and Nancy (Nanny) Priestley. James and Nanny settled in Bradford while Ely and William remained in Halifax, where they each raised their families. Betty and Maria were close and supportive to each other. Betty was particularly sad when Maria died in childbirth in 1828. William and Betty had ten children, but like so many couples, at the time, not all of these children survived into adulthood. Like Adam and Eve, William and Betty had sons, Cain and Abel, but these two brothers were not rivals nor rebellious, growing up together and remaining close into adulthood.

Ely and William's sons, Joseph and Thomas worked together in the quarries around Halifax. By the end of the nineteenth century, Halifax had hundreds of mills built from this stone. Joseph and Thomas met sisters, Elizabeth and Grace Broadbent in Halifax. Thomas married Elizabeth in 1835 and Joseph married Grace in 1839. Short time, unemployment, strikes and illness had always had a mercurial effect on the life chances of the working class. People like the Priestley's had to move around searching for work, so in the 1840's Joseph and Grace moved to Bradford.

Joseph and Grace

Joseph Priestley and Grace Broadbent were married on the 7th December 1839. They lived at Lilley Lane in Halifax close to the open-air swimming pool and public baths built in the 1750's It was here that baby William was born in 1841 but died in 1845. Samuel was baptised in 1842 and Abraham was born on 12th October 1844 when the family lived at Copley Hall in the Skircoat township of Halifax. Copley Hall was an old farmhouse in Copley village, originally the Manor of Copley, dating back many centuries. Joseph and several other families shared the farmhouse. Their living conditions were cramped and unsanitary in contrast to the model village that Edward Akroyd was building around them.

Akroyd owned a large mill in the village of Copley in 1847. Behind the mill he had built an estate of terrace cottages, for his workers. He also provided his workers with a library, school and canteen. Men like Akroyd, Titus Salt of Saltaire near Bradford, successful Victorian businessmen, felt it their Christian duty to provide for their workforce. They were true philanthropists who spent thousands of pounds on improving the living conditions of their fellow men. Sadly, Edward Akroyd did not employ Joseph so he and his family could not benefit from the houses being built around them. He and Grace decided to move to Bradford where there was plenty of work in the quarries.

In 1853 Joseph, Grace and their children, Samuel, Abraham, Sarah-Ann and Mary Hannah lived at Dick Lane, Pudsey near Bradford. Elizabeth was born in 1854 but Grace was not assisted in her labour by the administration of chloroform. Dr. John Snow, a Yorkshire man, had given Queen Victoria a little chloroform during the birth of her eighth child, Prince Leopold in 1853. The social elite of London, followed the Queen's lead in this method of anaesthesia, but the majority of women had no pain relief. Their day-to-day lives were dominated by labour and pain, childbirth was just toil to bear.

Joseph worked in one of Bradford's many quarries. Mills, houses and public building were filling the town as this was an era of civic pride in most wealthy woollen towns. Town halls, churches, theatres and concert halls were built in towns like Bradford. St. George's Hall, the concert hall, was opened in 1853. It was here that Charles Dickens appeared to give a recital, but not to men like Joseph Priestley. The average working man could not have afforded a ticket. In 1857 Joseph died at his home at Dick Lane, he was forty-seven years old. Grace was left with five children, and almost destitute. Every morning as the sun was rising, Grace would take the long pole, which she kept by her door and knock on the bedroom window of all those who needed to be woken, to go to their work in the mills. Very few people could tell the time, let alone afford to buy a timepiece. Women like Grace were essential members of the community. Workers depended upon her to waken them. If they were late for work their pay was reduced. Grace and the children where a whisker away from admission to the workhouse.

Abraham and Emma

After the family moved to Bradford from Halifax, Abraham and Sam worked in the coalmines. Children were small, agile and dexterous workers underground, just as they were above ground in the mills, performing tasks the adults could not, yet being paid less for doing so. The work was dirty and dangerous and not the place for young children. Both boys and girls were employed in the mines in and around Yorkshire. The children's income was essential to poor, working class families, so the work continued until legislation was introduced to change these working practices. Sam and Abraham's income was essential to Grace after Joseph's death.

In 1866 Sarah-Ann, Abraham's sister, married George Tetley. One year later, Abraham married Emma, George's sister. Abraham and Emma lived with his mother Grace and his sisters at Dick Lane. This was a busy, overcrowded home with happy and sad memories. Emma and Abraham had nine children Sam, Elizabeth, Clara, Mary-Ann, Joseph, Eliza, Henrietta, Alfred and Grace, named after Abraham's mother. Grace was born on 15th June 1885 her birthday, a few years later was to be a most memorable one.

Elizabeth Priestley

Like her brother Abraham, Elizabeth was born in Halifax. She was born in 1854 when the family lived at Copley Hall. After moving to Bradford she and her sister, Mary Hannah, went to school part-time and then worked together in a worsted mill. Bradford was known as the 'worsted capital of the world' and bore the title 'Worstedopolis'. This high quality cloth was exported around the world and clothed and furnished the people and their homes in Britain. There were those, however, who could not afford such a fabric and they were the people who were responsible for its manufacture. Mary Hannah and Elizabeth would have worn woollen shawls, long skirts and wooden clogs in summer and winter- time. All working class people wore clogs. The noise these clogs made on the stone steps of the mills, must have been deafening, with use and time the clogs slowly deformed each step in the mills.

Like so many mill workers Elizabeth spent much of her time at work, there was little time for leisure. Elizabeth met Isaac Naylor whilst working in the mill. Isaac was a 'twister' at the mill. This was a process in worsted weaving. They married and in 1881 they lived at Broad Lane, Laisterdyke in Bradford and had four children, Mary, Herbert, Oliver and Violet. Later, they moved to Wilberforce Street, named after William Wilberforce the anti-slave campaigner. Sarah-Ann, Martha, Ethel and Broadbent were born here. Broadbent was named after Elizabeth's mother. These children took the same route to the mills as Elizabeth and her family had, until the world was turned upside down by war.

The Millmasters

The Bottomley Family

There had been many generations of Bottomleys living in Shelf in the West Riding throughout the eighteenth and nineteenth centuries. 'Wade House' (see figure 16) was their family home. Samuel Bottomley inherited the family worsted mill, in Shelf with his brother, Moses. He took full control of the manufacturing there in the 1870's. Samuel married Caroline Jane Holmes, from Pocklington near York, in 1853. Her father was the local solicitor and her maternal grandfather was the Rev. William Cautley of Bishop Wilton, also near York.

Samuel and Caroline lived at Ann Place in the fashionable part of Horton in Bradford after their marriage. It was here that twins Caroline Constance and Sarah Elizabeth were born in 1854. Florence Jane was born in 1855 followed by Moses Nathaniel in 1857 and Cautley Holmes in 1858. It was Caroline's family's wish that her children be given their family names. They moved to Westbrook House, also in Horton, where Samuel and Caroline planned the building of their next home, Shelf Hall, (often later to be known as "New Shelf Hall"), near Samuel's mill and the existing old Shelf Hall. J.T.Fairbank probably designed the house in 1860 at a building cost of almost £40,000. His design was of a magnificent mansion in the Italianate style, two storeys high, heavily baroque with a pediment to the garden front, supported on grand Corinthian columns with urns and balustrading above the corners of the house. It overlooked the valley of Lightcliffe with Coley church to its right. The land on which it was built was owned by the Priestley family, but had come into the hands of the Bottomley's through a succession of trustees.

Samuel became one of Yorkshire's 'Captains of Industry' like many successful worsted manufacturers in the nineteenth century, evidence of the Yorkshire adage 'where there's muck, there's brass'. Sadly, baby Caroline Constance died in 1854 and

Caroline died in 1859. Caroline never lived in Shelf Hall. Their sons boarded at a school in Sedbergh in Westmorland. Nathaniel and Cautley went up to Oxford to read law and later became barristers in London, neither had a wish to join the wool trade. Sarah and Florence married worsted manufacturers, Albert and Rufus Mitchell, two other 'Captains of Industry' from Bowling in Bradford. On 24th June 1883 Samuel died at his home in Shelf he was sixty-four years old. Because he died intestate, Nathaniel his eldest son inherited the hall, mill and property in Shelf and Bradford. In 1885 Nathaniel and Cautley changed their surnames, by Royal Licence, to Cautley. They were required to do so as beneficiaries of a will, made by a member of their mother's family.

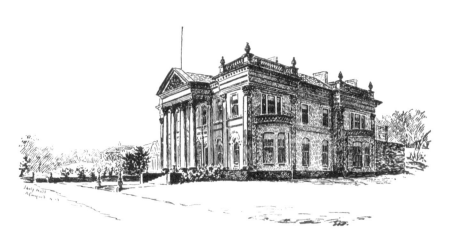

Figure 15. Shelf Hall (Drawing by Arthur Cumfort).

The Heir-at-Law

John Edwin Priestley

Born in 1865, John was Joseph and Catherine's eldest son. Bradford at this time was made up of a warp and weft society of migrants from rural areas of England and Ireland. His mother had arrived from Ireland in the 1840's. His parents had suffered great hardship prior to his birth, his mother and sisters had been paupers in the workhouse and his father had been in and out of work. When John was four years old his mother was admitted to the Lunatic Asylum where she later died, he probably grew up with few memories of her. His father re-married in 1875 when Ann became his stepmother. John became yet another 'worker' in Bradford's 'hive of industry' at one of the many woollen mills. John had often listened to his father talk about James Priestley's will and how, through the male line his family should have inherited Shelf Hall Farm estate. However, through a succession of trustees the land had been lost to the Bottomleys. In 1881 when his father died, John realised that he was the heir-at-law to the estate, but since his grandfather and father had failed to successfully claim the property, he felt that as a poor, humble working class lad, it was unlikely he would, so he made other plans.

In the eighteenth century Joseph Priestley, a forebear of John's settled in County Durham where he established a branch of the Priestley family. In the mid 1880's John boarded a train from Bradford to Middlesbrough, were he settled with the descendents of Joseph Priestley. Middlesbrough, like Bradford, at the time, had attracted many immigrants. The town's railway, iron and steel and mining industries were booming. Gladstone described Middlesbrough as the 'infant Hercules'. John had no difficulty in finding a job and very soon found a wife.

On the 5th June 1888 John married Mary Jane Leng, the daughter of a seaman. On 11th July 1889 Mary Jane gave birth to

Ernest. John enlisted in the militia in 1890 and settled down to married life in Middlesbrough, but the family, back home in Bradford, did not share John's reticence in the claim to Shelf Hall. They were busy establishing the 'Priestley Syndicate'. This was the beginning of the fight, through the courts for Shelf Hall. Shelf Hall had become their 'Bleak House' and they were the 'Jarndyce and Jarndyce' of the day.

The 'Priestley Litigation'

Generations of Priestleys had grown up with the story of their claim to Shelf Hall and as a result a movement developed among the Priestley clan. Joseph Priestley, the living descendent of James Priestley, at the time had, in 1869, along with his brothers John (Jack) and Benjamin (Jem), pulled down a tree on the land owned by Samuel Bottomley. It was a desperate attempt at 'pretension to ownership of the estate', they were prosecuted for the act by Samuel and made to pay a fine of £1.0.0 each or go to gaol. They paid the fine.

Rebecca, Joseph's sister, was passionate about the family's claim to the estate, she was determined to prove their legitimate claim to the land despite the fact that they were poor people and lacked the funds to fight their claim through Chancery. Rebecca would make formal objections at the sale of property Mr. Cautley put up for auction, claiming it belonged to her family. On the 26th July 1887 an auction of the Shelf Hall Estate property was held in Halifax. Nathaniel Cautley had arranged for thirty lots to be auctioned. Shelf Hall Farm, the mansion, Shelf Hall and other farms and cottages were included. Rebecca often attended the auctions Nathaniel held. She had become a 'cause célèbre' at these auctions because of her objections to the sales and her claim to ownership of the estate. On this day, Rebecca stood up and in anger and determination, warned any prospective buyers that they would purchase the property at their peril. Mr Lupton, Nathaniel's solicitor was also present and he chided her on her attendance at auctions and said 'he hoped she might long be spared to lend zest and interest to auction sales.' He sarcastically accused her of 'claiming the whole country side' Rebecca disregarded his comments and witnessed thirteen of the thirty lots being sold, but Shelf Hall Farm and the mansion Shelf Hall were not sold.

She regularly sought advice, for their claim, from solicitors in Bradford, Leeds and London. Her vigour and determination enthused many friends and supporters. In 1888 Rebecca, John, Abraham and his sister Elizabeth and Albert formed a syndicate of willing financial supporters. They became known as the 'Priestley Syndicate'. The aim of the syndicate was to 'contest the title of the owner (Nathaniel Cautley) of the estate to retain possession' through the High Court.

The estate was made up of Shelf Hall, the mansion built by Samuel Bottomley at a cost of £40,000, a large mill, Shelf Hall Farm and other farms and cottages, to the value of £500,000. At the time of the proceedings John Edwin Priestley, the heir-at-law to the estate, was working as an engine tenter at a works in Silsbridge Lane in Bradford. Mr. Johnson a member of the syndicate visited John there and said to him, 'Will you give me your consent to go on with the case?'

John replied, 'Certainly, if you think you can get it.'

'I will try', confirmed Mr. Johnson.

Three weeks or a month elapsed when John was working in a moulder's shop in Middlesbrough. Mr. Ellis, who was acting on behalf of the syndicate, visited him. Mr. Ellis had good news for John. The claim had been successful. He said to John, 'Put on thi coit, lad, thahs done workin'. John was given £1.0.0 per week and promised that the estate would be his in a fortnight.

Mr. Ellis took John to a gentleman's outfitters, where he purchased a silk hat and suit of broad cloth for John. They travelled to Shelf where they met the Sheriff of Yorkshire's officer, Mr Gaunt, who had been instructed to put John in possession of the estate, under an order of the High Court of Justice. 'An antique and singular ceremony was performed, whereby they went on the land, in Shelf, having carefully ascertained what fields were composed in the order which he held. Mr Gaunt dug up a green sod with a pearl-handed penknife and handed it to Mr. Ellis, who received it on John's behalf.' Mr. Ellis slapped John on his back and said 'Thah'll work noo more lad.' John felt a 'proper swell' in possession of fine clothes and an estate valued at £500,000.

A short time later, the judgement of writ of possession was set aside for irregularities and Mr. Cautley was re-instated in possession of the estate. The irregularities were as a result of the notice of appeal being given two days late, or rather; the notice was given within the requisite eight days, but should have been set down on the sixth day. It was a technical point, a clerk's blunder that cost John his inheritance. John returned to Middlesbrough with his silk hat and suit of broad cloth, a poor man once again.

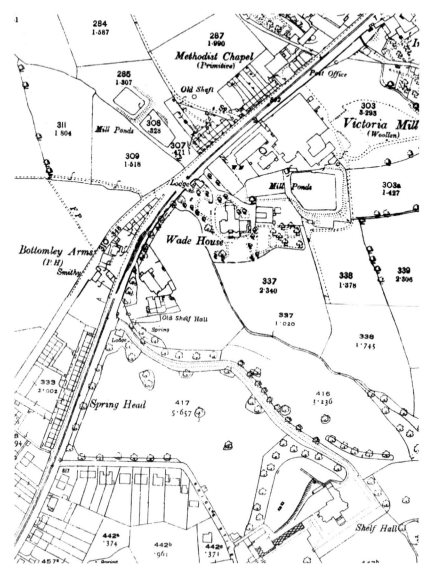

Figure 16. Map of 1933 showing the two Shelf Halls, Wade House and Bottomley's Mill. (By kind permission of Bradford Central Library).

55

The Occupation of Shelf Hall

Days of Action

The 'Priestley Litigation' of 1888 was not the end of the Priestley's fight for the estate. Rebecca Crellin was determined she and several members of her family would pursue their claim, even if John did not want to join them. Abraham, Albert, Maria and Elizabeth often met in Rebecca's shop on Cavendish Street in Leeds to discuss the litigation and the 'clerk's blunder' which made Rebecca so angry. In May 1893 they met again at Rebecca's shop to discuss a plan of action. It had been five and a half years since the litigation and they had until February 1894 to contest the title of the estate, before they were barred by the 'Statute of Limitations'. Rebecca would not 'let the sand run out!' They decided to occupy Mr. Cautley's home, Shelf Hall.

Figure 17.
Shelf Hall Lodge, the home of caretakers Jonathan and Alice Holmes.

The 12th June 1893 was to be the big day. Two weeks before the planned occupation, Rebecca went to the hall to see Mr. Cautley, with the aim of telling him her intentions, but he was not there. Her motive for doing this is not apparent, but it is perhaps fortunate for her that Mr. Cautley was not there, for almost certainly, there would have been a defensive reception party waiting for them on the day of the proposed occupation. The hall had not been lived in for ten years, but Mr. Woodhead, who lived near the hall, acted as the agent for the estate. Jonathan and Alice Holmes, an elderly couple who were caretakers of the hall, lived in the lodge near the entrance, and had a sitting room in the hall. Rebecca told them her intentions.

Monday 12th June 1893

Rebecca, Abraham, Elizabeth, Maria and her husband George Cooper, met in Bradford. They travelled in the tramcar the five miles, from Bradford to Shelf terminus, reaching there at 10am to meet several other members of the Priestley family, including Albert. There were about fourteen people in total. The entrance to the hall, through an ornamental recessed gateway was only a few yards from the terminus. The lodge, where the caretaker lived, was to the right of the gateway. The Priestley party walked down the carriage drive, leading to the hall and vista beyond. The view from the front of the hall looked onto the beautiful valley of Lightcliffe and the Derbyshire hills, in the distance.

The house was a magnificent mansion built in the classical style, in extensive parkland. There was a large conservatory, vinery and peach house, but these had been left to decay. The carriage drive was overgrown with weeds and the grass had grown knee high. The whole house and parkland had an air of neglect and desolation. As the house was unoccupied, at the time, Rebecca and her party had no difficulty gaining access. Mr. Holmes, the caretaker had seen them walking down the drive, but it was impossible for him to stop them. All he could do was to inform Mr. Cautley's solicitor, Mr. Lupton from Messrs. Lupton

Figure 18. Present-day view from the position of Shelf Hall front door with Coley Church tower to be seen between the two similar trees.

and Fawcett of Leeds, that they were in situ.

Abraham, Albert and George investigated the stables and yard at the rear of the house and found some coals these would be useful if they needed a fire. Rebecca, Maria and Elizabeth unpacked the things they had brought to sustain them throughout the siege. They were surprised to find that there was very little furniture in the house; only the caretaker's room was furnished. They walked from room to room in amazement.

The entrance hall gave access to the drawing room, dining room, breakfast room, library, billiard room and housekeeper's room. The ceilings and cornices were veritable works of art with moulded and a gilded ornament of bunches of grapes and pineapples. The dining room was the finest room with panelled walls. A large stained-glass window lighted the staircase; the balusters of the stairs were made of imitation sheaves of wheat.

In front of the landing was a carved representation of a sports man in the act of firing with a dog in advance. There were two dressing rooms, two bathrooms and two lavatories. The bedrooms were large and lofty, but dirty. Rebecca was keen to point out the cobwebs to Elizabeth and Maria. The main rooms were fitted with electric lights. From the thirty rooms in the house, they chose the library as their headquarters.

During the evening several members of the public visited the hall, keen to see the invaders and the inside and outside of the hall. Many were workers from Bottomley's mill, others were members of the family anxious to see the extent of the estate.

Tuesday 13th June 1893

Rebecca, Abraham, Albert and Elizabeth remained at the hall and the rest of Monday's party left. Rebecca felt that the four of them could secure the house from Mr Cautley's representatives. However, Mr Lupton's clerk visited the house to ask for the names and addresses of those who lay claim to the estate, with the intention of applying, in London, for an order 'restraining them from remaining in possession of the hall or interfering with Mr. Cautley's possession of the premises'. This was just what the Priestleys wanted. Their claim to the estate would be highlighted once again and would then have to be tried before the courts.

Albert gave the clerk their names and addresses: Rebecca Crellin formerly Brown nee Priestley, Cavendish Street, Leeds; Abraham Priestley, Dick Lane, Dudley Hill, Bradford; Elizabeth Naylor nee Priestley, Swain Green, Bradford; Albert Priestley, Gibbet Lane, Halifax. He was polite and co-operative to the clerk. Rebecca had insisted they showed some 'breeding', after all their ancestors had been Lords and Ladies. He hoped the newspapers would hear of their situation and print their story this would give them the publicity they needed to pursue their cause. He wished that their present action would be the final chapter in the Priestley story. Albert admired aunt 'Becca's' passion and commitment, she was their 'tour de force' but whilst the other party were well educated, wealthy, with legal minds, aunt 'Becca could neither read nor write.

Once again, many local people gathered at the hall to see the Priestley clan. People walked up and down the carriage drive investigating the stables and admiring the house, internally and externally. In fact, the house and grounds were crowded with people, some of the crowd showed sympathy for their cause, others felt loyalty to the Bottomley family, although many did not know Nathaniel Cautley, nor that he had changed his name. There were those, in the village, who knew of the Priestley's claim to the estate and that there had been many generations of Priestleys in Shelf. Rebecca took advantage of the crowd's interest and knowledge of her family and she eagerly answered their questions, whilst escorting them around the grounds. When the sightseers left the hall, those in the family who were to stay the night, settled down in the library. They had enough provisions to last them at least a week.

Wednesday 14th June 1893

Many more family, friends and sightseers visited the hall. Susannah and David Nichol, from Queensbury visited them in the evening. Like Rebecca and the other claimants, Susannah was also a descendent of James Priestley. She and David were as passionate as they were, to prove the claim to the estate. For more than twenty years David had spent every penny he could scrape together in getting legal advice in the matter. He was subjected, as a consequence, to a good deal of banter by those aware of his proceedings, but he never lost faith in the legitimate character of the claim. Although Susannah was three years older than Rebecca, they were particularly close, having grown up together during the turbulent years of Victoria's reign. Susannah affectionately called Rebecca 'Becky'. Although devoid of the culture of Thackeray's heroine, Becky Sharp, Rebecca was equally sharp and cunning.

Becky showed Susannah around the house, neither of them

had ever seen such a grand house. They stood at the front door of the mansion. Becky was wearing a light bodice with a cream coloured silk handkerchief tied loosely around her neck, a dark skirt and an apron. She wore a wedding ring and two dress rings, one on her right hand. They looked up above the doorway at the tympanum bearing the arms of the Bottomleys. This was a shield, on which was a lion rampant and two bees on which bore the motto 'FIDELI CERTA MERCES' surrounded by a goat standing beneath a tree. Although it looked impressive neither knew its meaning. They walked into the entrance hall and on the ceiling were a number of scripture texts and mottos. In bold letters were written 'The strong may fail and the weak succeed' and 'Oil quells storms'. Had they been able to read they may have seen the significance of the text, in light of the current situation.

David and Susannah left the hall with the other sightseers. Rebecca, Elizabeth and Albert stayed 'on duty' in the hall. Abraham returned home.

Thursday 15th June 1893

This was Grace's birthday she was eight years old. Abraham had promised he would take her to the hall. Grace and her father took the tramcar to Shelf. It seemed such a long way and took a long time to get there. But it was a lovely day and the sun was shining. They walked down the carriage drive to the hall, which was to Grace, almost as big as the town hall in Bradford, but much nicer and cleaner. She had never seen a house surrounded by fields before and there were daisies growing among the grass. She could see a church, with a tower, in the distance. At the side of the house, but not attached to it was a conservatory and a vinery. Grace did not know what a vinery was. She and Abraham looked inside and saw all the vines dead and withered. On those that were still showing signs of feeble life, last year's grapes were dried and decayed. Grace thought that if that was what grapes looked like, she never wanted to eat them. Close by was the peach house, with most of the limbs of the tree decayed and

Figure 19. The surviving stable block of Shelf Hall.

lifeless, here and there were a few pinched and starved looking peaches struggling to exist. Everything seemed to be dead or dying. The conservatory was a large glasshouse she and Abraham walked inside, but it too, was bare. Grace did not know that Samuel Bottomley had been found dead in the conservatory some ten years earlier. Abraham took Grace to the back of the house where the stables were. He told her that once they owned Shelf Hall, they would have a 'coach and pair' and she could have a horse of her own. Grace looked around the dirty stable yard. There was grass and weeds and a young sycamore growing out of the cracks. Then suddenly a longtail appeared among a heap of stones and stared at her, as much as to say 'What are you doing in my snug quarters?' She had seen lots of longtails at home but she did not expect to see them here. Grace was not sure she liked Shelf Hall.

In the house, aunt Becky had a visitor. The reporter from the 'Bradford Daily Argus' newspaper was the 'first on the scene' at the hall, with the intention of interviewing Rebecca. Newspaper coverage was just what Rebecca wanted. Hopefully, their story would be reported around Yorkshire and the capital. He began by asking her 'Who made the will under which this dispute has arisen?'

Rebecca answered. 'Our great grandfather, James Priestley, he lived at Shelf Hall Farm and that he owned all the property, the tenants paying their rents at the Duke William Hotel. That was before this house was built. The boxes belonging to the Priestley family were at the Duke William but after the family became beneficiaries under the will, they gave notice of an intention to take possession, but the boxes were removed'

'Was that before the litigation?' he asked.

Rebecca said 'Yes, before. We sold some cottages at Buttershaw and got the money for them. Our lawyer told the purchaser that we were the rightful owners, although we were poor. He said our pedigree goes to the Lords and Ladies of the Manor of Wibsey and Shelf and that our pedigree went back through three courts and we were not disputed, we lost simply by a small technical point, a clerk's blunder'

His next question was 'What about the young John Priestley who is descended as the heir-at-law?'

Rebecca's voice became raised as she said, 'We don't want anything to do with him. We don't want to own him.'

She was asked, 'You, yourself claim to have a share in the benefit. Who are you and those who are with you in asserting this right or possession?'

Rebecca's reply was, 'Yes, under the will of James, Joseph and Jonathan we are one out of every family concerned.'

Rebecca began to talk about Nathaniel Cautley. She had been in dispute with him for many years. She told the reporter that he called her a deluded woman and this made her angry.

'Deluded woman! That means I am wrong in my head and

there is always protection for wrong headed women, you know.'
'See here,' she said. After being absent for a few moments she returned and said. 'Somebody, has sent us this leg of mutton, we're not going to pine.'

After this outbreak by Rebecca, the reporter felt he must calm the situation, so he asked her about her arrival on Monday. Rebecca told him that the caretaker was in charge of the premises when they arrived. She went on to say 'Well, the caretaker's wife was in bed on Monday and it was said she was too ill to be moved. So we told them they could stay a few days'

'But', said the reporter 'What if they on the other side are content with their caretaker being in possession and are now applying for an injunction to restrain you from taking possession?'

'By gow!' exclaimed Rebecca. 'That's what they are doing and that's what they mean by sending their lawyer every day. But I'll go and tell the caretaker to go out at once.'

Rebecca raced off to tell the caretaker and his wife to leave. After a while she returned and said. 'They refuse to go but they'll have to leave today. I'll have no more of their technical points.'

The reporter went on to ask 'Are you well prepared to withstand an attempt to break in and re-enter into possession by Mr. Cautley?'

'Yes we are that, we are well supported with provisions, which we got in on Tuesday morning. We can stand out some time, though as yet no attempt to enter has been made' she said.

'If an attempt is made to enter do you mean force?' he asked.

'Yes, just you see if we don't. All the windows are fastened and the doors barred and if any man comes in I'll settle him with this poker what ever the consequences are' she said as she hammered large nails into the windows and doors, making the house as secure as possible.

He asked, 'Have you seen Mr. Cautley?'

'No, he is in London taking steps to obtain an injunction against us and if that is so we shall then raise our title in the court properly. That is what we want; we are sure we can win', replied Rebecca.

He went on to ask. 'Are you provided with firearms or a continual supply of hot water?'

'No, cold steel nothing but steel' she said as she waved the poker in the air.

'Are you fully determined not to let anyone in and take possession?' he asked.

'Yes we are, no one comes in but over my body', she answered.

'What kinds of helpers have you in case of attack?' the reporter asked.

Rebecca thought for a while and then said, 'Well some of us are game enough; but one or two don't seem to realise the importance of the matter and stand around like 'sucking ducks''

'Will they show fight?' he asked.

She continued hammering more nails into the window frame and with one final bang said, 'I'll cleaver the skull of the person that dares to try and get in.'

The reporter made a hasty retreat.

Rebecca sent Abraham and her nephew to Leeds to see their solicitor, Mr. Iveson, to obtain his advice.

Grace was quite afraid of aunt Becky's behaviour, she stayed close to aunt Elizabeth and her baby, Ethel. She had never had a birthday like this before.

Shortly after Abraham had left the hall, Rebecca saw Mr. Lupton, Mr. Cautley's solicitor, his clerk and half a dozen bailiffs, walking towards the house. He knocked on the door, but got no response. Rebecca went to the kitchen window, joined by Elizabeth and then Mr. Holmes, the caretaker. A bat and ball dialogue between Rebecca and Mr. Lupton ensued:

Mr. Lupton said, 'let me in, in the name of the law.'

Rebecca said, 'In the name of the law, stop outside.'

Mr. Lupton responded with, 'If you don't let me in I shall force my way.'

Rebecca said, 'Do it then and I'll crack the neck of the first man that comes in here.'

Mr. Lupton said to the caretaker, 'Open the door, can't you? It's only a woman that hinders you.'

Rebecca said excitedly, 'It's a woman that can hinder him.'

Mr. Lupton again to Mr. Holmes, 'Open the door caretaker.'

Rebecca's response was, 'He can't do it.'

Mr. Lupton said in anger, 'I'll smash in the window.'

Rebecca said, 'Smash it and I'll smash your head with this (waving a poker) I'll murder the first man that enters.'

In quieter tones Mr. Lupton said, 'Well, open the window I want to serve you a writ.' Rebecca slowly opened the window, just wide enough to put her basket through. She told Mr. Lupton to put the writ in the basket. She raised the basket and pulled it in through the window whilst telling Mr. Lupton and the bailiffs to leave the hall.

Mr. Lupton, his clerk and the bailiffs walked round to the front of the house. Mr. Lupton tried the front door and found it open. He and his clerk and a couple of bailiffs walked inside, only to find Rebecca whizzing across the hall in their direction. She seized Mr. Lupton by the neck and hurled him down the steps. All the men landed in a heap at the bottom of the steps. Rebecca slammed the door shut and hammered more nails into the floor. Mr. Lupton, like the reporter, made a hasty retreat.

The clerk and bailiffs were left in charge. Their intention was to gain entry to the hall, but in the mean time, they set up their headquarters in the conservatory.

Various people from Shelf and the surrounding area visited the hall to see what was happening. But this time Rebecca did not allow anyone inside. She spoke to people through the window, mainly by raising her voice and gesticulating in answer to their questions. She explained that she had been summoned to the High Court of Justice; Chancery Division, in London, the following day. An injunction was to be obtained restraining Albert, Abraham, Elizabeth and Rebecca from remaining in possession of Shelf Hall, or otherwise interfering with the possession of Mr. Cautley. Although they had all been summoned, it was decided that Rebecca would attend. She hoped to apply for an adjournment of the hearing on the grounds that they had not had time to prepare any defence to the summons.

Someone in the crowd asked her when she would leave for London. She said she would send Albert and Abraham to Halifax to borrow the money for her journey to London. Then she would take the train to Bradford and book at the Midland station. She hoped to get the early morning train, reaching St. Pancras shortly after eight o'clock. Her main concern was how she would vacate the hall without the bailiffs gaining access. So concerned was she, that she seriously thought of lowering herself by means of a rope from one of the bedrooms.

There was a great deal of banter between Rebecca and the bailiffs. They were polite, but mistrusted each other. An elderly gentleman who had some connection with the estate walked into the courtyard. He exchanged pleasantries with the bailiffs. Rebecca saw him and said, 'Ye out to be ashamed or yersen. You've one fut i't grave an't'other aht; where do you expect to go tull when yu dee'

To which he replied, 'I don't want to go where you are going.' 'Noa' she retorted 'Ah'll se thah doen't.'

Rebecca left the window and the bailiffs began to patrol the grounds and the sightseers, having felt satisfactorily entertained left the hall.

Some time later Rebecca heard a noise at the front door. Thinking that perhaps it was Abraham and Albert returning she went to look. It was, in fact, two of the bailiffs. They had secured the two front door knobs with wire.

Rebecca said to Elizabeth. 'They're trying to push t'front door oppin, but by gow! If thew dew I'll smash t'head of t' first man at enters.'

At ten o'clock Albert and Abraham returned from Halifax with the necessary funds for Rebecca's trip to London. There was a scuffle between the bailiffs, Albert and Abraham regarding gaining access to the hall. Eventually, it was decided to allow the bailiffs entry. They were allocated their own room and told to remain there. The Priestley party was given instructions not to leave the hall. Rebecca left at eleven o'clock.

Fortunately, it was market day in Bradford, so there was a late tramcar to Bankfoot. Rebecca walked from Bankfoot to the station in Bradford, reaching there at almost midnight. She had £2.10.0 for her trip to the Metropolis.

Friday 16th June 1893

High Court of Justice. Chancery Division
Cautley v Crellin

Rebecca was familiar with the hustle and bustle of Leeds, but nothing could have prepared her for her trip to London. The city was crowded with people, most of who were rushing around. She saw men and women wearing the strangest of clothes. They all seemed to speak a foreign language. As she could not read the street signs she had to ask passers-by for directions. However, they could not understand her West Riding dialect and she could not understand their reply. She thought they were the most ignorant people she had ever met. A policeman directed her to Chancery Lane. Rebecca found herself 'In Chancery' after all the years of staking their claim.

His Lordship, Mr. Justice Sterling was a nice man, she thought. He asked her name. She stood up in the courtroom and in a loud voice said, 'Rebecca Crellin.' She asked if he would give her permission for a few more days in order to allow her to answer the evidence. He agreed. She was delighted things were going her way, until Mr. Warrington, the counsel for Mr. Cautley said, 'His Lordship could not, for a moment, allow the present state of things to continue at Shelf Hall.' Too true, Rebecca thought. Mr. Cautley should be told to hand the estate over immediately.

However, Mr. Justice Sterling did grant an ex parte injunction until Tuesday 'to restrain the defendants from excluding the plaintiff and all persons authorised by him from Shelf Hall' but declined to say that the defendants were not entitled to be at the hall until the defendants had had an opportunity of answering the evidence. So Rebecca and the rest of the family could stay for the time being.

Rebecca made her way back to the railway station, very pleased to be returning north, to Yorkshire, 'God's own County'.

Saturday 17th June 1893

Rebecca did not return from the hearing, in London until after midnight. She had walked from Bradford to Shelf. When she reached the hall, she rapped on the window. Albert came to the window and said, 'They have ordered me not to open the door' Rebecca was livid, she said to Albert. 'Open it, or I'll put my foot to a panel and open it myself.' In fear of the bailiffs, but more so of Rebecca, Albert let her in. Rebecca said, 'If they ever say that again, they must 'pick their windows''

The bailiffs and Rebecca exchanged heated words but settled down for the night. Later in the day, Rebecca left the hall to visit her husband and her solicitor in Leeds. She and her solicitor were to prepare affidavits to present before Mr Justice Sterling on Tuesday in the High Court.

Sunday 18th June 1893

Several members of the Priestley family and their friends visited the hall in the morning. After hearing about this from Mr Woodhead the agent, Mr. Lupton the solicitor visited the hall. He arranged for a lock and chain to be attached to the gate, to prevent people entering the estate. When Rebecca saw the lock she was angry. She ordered Abraham and Albert to remove it. She said to Mr. Woodhead. 'Who put this lock on?'

'I did', said Mr. Woodhead

'If you do this again without my permission, I will put you on the gate.' Rebecca exclaimed.

Mr. Woodhead left the hall in despair.

After the removal of the lock and chain, the crowds gathered outside the gate and inside the grounds. There were hundreds of people from Bradford, Halifax and Shelf. This seemed an ideal opportunity to raise funds for their cause from the crowd. The Hull dockers, in their recent strike, had raised money in this way. Rebecca decided that they would do the same. One member of the family was stationed at the gate with a collection box, collecting money from sightseers and passers-by. She carried a cigar box among the crowds in the grounds. She rattled it occasionally to show how rapidly it was filling.

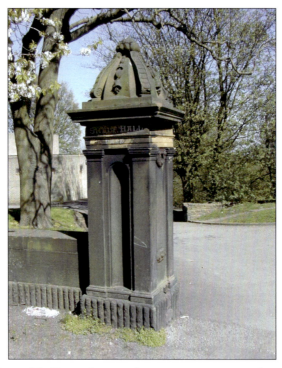

Figure 20. Ornately carved entrance gate-post where money was collected for the Priestley cause.

Mr. Lupton arranged for a policeman to be stationed at the entrance gates to keep order, but as the grounds were so extensive, it was an impossible task. Many people found their way to the front of the hall without being seen by the policeman. Sergeant Metcalf's officers, from the West Riding Constabulary, remained in their post at the hall for several days.

As the evening drew on, the sightseers left the hall. Only a small band of family and friends remained. Rebecca invited them into the upper floor of the house, for a meeting. Abraham, Albert and the other male members of the family discussed their claim and answered questions. Shortly after the family left, the head bailiff ventured to show a few of his friends around. Rebecca heard his party and stormed into the room. She ordered them down the stairs and then, promptly pounced on the bailiff, ultimately pushing him down the stairs. Neither the bailiffs nor the Priestleys slept well that night.

Monday 19th June 1893

The reporter from the 'Bradford Observer' newspaper visited the hall in the morning. He saw three bailiffs 'lounging about their quarters' whilst at the rear of the hall the Priestleys were busy sawing wood. Rebecca explained to the reporter what they planned to do, saying,

'This morning after we had our breakfast, we thought the best way would be to build a place of our own on our ground, so that if they get their injunction tomorrow, we can remove on to our ground. About half past eight I took a spade and took up a sod and then the men went on digging for the posts. We are going to put up a dwelling place.'

Their intention was to occupy the hall as long as possible without an infringement of the law and then move to a temporary building and assent a claim to the ground. Rebecca expected that the injunction, which was applied for, would be granted in respect of the hall, but they meant to hold on to the land. There was no doubt that Rebecca was determined to continue to assert her right to the estate. After the reporter left, Rebecca supervised the erection of the wooden hut. She stood, with arms akimbo, giving instructions, firstly to Albert, then Abraham.

Later in the day, the reporter from the 'Halifax Mercury' newspaper turned up, keen to be shown around. Rebecca threw open the front door and invited him in. Rebecca held out a cigar box in front of him, in anticipation of a donation towards their claim. The reporter dropped a silver coin into the box. He was shown the nails she had driven into the floor, close to the door to keep out the 'bums'. With a touch of humour in her voice she said, 'Now, sir, I will sell you the hall at a moderate figure. Are you inclined to buy?' He declined her invitation and followed her into a room. She turned around suddenly and said, 'We have done very well for our collection. We're not going to be beat. If the lawyers turn us out of the hall we will camp on the land and continue to assert our rights to an estate stolen from us.'

The reporter was introduced to Abraham and Albert who had just come indoors after building the wooden hut. Suddenly, out of the corner of her eye Rebecca noticed one of the 'bums' straying into a part of the hall which she considered to be hers. 'She pounced upon him and seized him by the hair of his head in a language more forcible than polite, boxed his ears, slapped his face and hustled him into his own quarters. The 'bum' was so astonished that he fled in dismay from the virago.'

The reporter was transfixed. He had never seen a woman with such physical strength and strength of character. The Suffragettes would have welcomed her in their cause. He wished her well in her endeavours and left the hall.

In the afternoon, Rebecca visited family in Halifax. A relative returned with her to Shelf in his trap.

Tuesday 20th June 1893

Chancery Division of the High Courts of Justice.
Mr. Justice Sterling had before him the case of Cautley v Crellin.

This is a motion by the plaintiff – Nathaniel Cautley – to restrain the defendants – Rebecca Crellin, Albert Priestley, Elizabeth Naylor and Abraham Priestley, their servants or agents from being in or upon any part of the messuage and hereditaments of the plaintiff known as Shelf Hall estate, in the County of York, or committing any acts of trespass thereon, or otherwise interfering with the possession of the plaintiff of the said messuage or hereditaments until the trial of the said action.

Mr. Warrington appeared for the plaintiff, Mr. Dickinson for the defendants, while Mr. Ford had a watching brief on behalf of some person interested.

Mr. Warrington, having reminded his Lordship that the matter was before him as recently as last Friday said the facts were these. Shelf Hall was a mansion, with a park and grounds attached. It was residential and situated near Bradford. The plaintiff, Mr. Cautley, and his father for forty years had been the owners and in possession of the estate. Mr. Cautley was not in personal occupation, but he had a caretaker in the house, and was therefore, legally in possession until last Monday, when the four defendants and a number of others came and broke into the house, and without turning out the caretaker encamped there and took up their abode. On Wednesday his Lordship gave him special leave to move on short notice on Friday. On Friday the defendants were represented by counsel, who asked for an adjournment in order that they might answer the plaintiff's affidavits. His Lordship granted the adjournment, at the same time making an ex-parte order restraining the defendants from excluding the plaintiffs or persons authorised by him from entrance to the estate and possession. He (Mr. Warrington) was instructed that at that time no appearance had been entered in the action, although the defendants were represented by counsel and solicitor. Immediately after his Lordship's order the solicitor was served with the notice stating what the affidavits were, and offering copies. No copies were taken, and not until that morning was appearance entered, when another solicitor entered it. He understood that his friend Mr. Dickinson was now instructed to ask for an adjournment. In these circumstances he asked his Lordship not to grant an adjournment. One of the defendants was in court on Friday, so that the facts were perfectly well known to the parties, and they further knew what had taken place. He ventured to say that the action of the defendants was simply a trick to obtain further time.

Mr. Justice Sterling: I notice Mr. Dickinson is not present. I can hardly deal with this in his absence.

Mr. Warrington: I understand he will be here in a moment.

Mr. Justice Sterling: Are they still in possession?

Mr. Warrington: I understand so, my Lord. If I may refer to the newspapers, it would appear that they are preparing to build themselves a hut in the courtyard, so that if they are turned out of the house, they can go in. I have an affidavit by a solicitor who went to the house on Tuesday and attempted to obtain possession. He was met by a lady with a long bar of iron, who threatened to kill him if he went into the house.

Mr. Dickinson: (who at this moment entered the court) said he had to ask his Lordship to allow the motion to stand over, at the same time containing the order made on Friday, and was represented by counsel, and it stood over in order that the affidavits might be answered. She was in London, and might have made an affidavit.

Mr. Ford: My Lord, I might say that I was instructed last Friday. I received my instructions in court. The solicitor who instructed me expected the lady to go to him yesterday to answer the affidavit.

Mr. Dickinson: I am instructed that the solicitor in Leeds did not receive their instructions until eight o'clock last night and I have only received my instructions at this moment. No harm could be done by an adjournment if the order was continued.

Mr. Warrington: I am told very great harm is being done. Hundreds of persons are being attracted by the proceedings and a great deal of harm is being done. I ask your Lordship to make the order. If my learned friend has any answer to my affidavit he can ask you to discharge the order.

Mr. Dickinson: I am in complete ignorance of what my friend is moving on. The order your Lordship has made is as complete a protection as any order your Lordship can make.

Mr. Justice Sterling: I don't take that view of the case. On the evidence before me they are simply trespassers.

Mr. Dickinson: Upon the face of the affidavits that would appear to be so; but I ask for an opportunity to meet them.

Mr. Justice Sterling: Certainly, more might have been done than has been done by your client. I made the order ex parte to prevent the defendants from excluding the plaintiff from possession, which he is entitled to do. It is obvious that if the statements in the affidavits are well founded a great deal of harm might be done.

Mr. Dickinson: Your Lordship is aware that this is a country case. The order was made on Friday so that notice would not be received until Saturday.

Mr. Justice Sterling: The defendant was in court and might have sworn an affidavit to show what prima-facie case she had. Her conduct is very extra-ordinary.

Mr. Dickinson: There are three defendants.

Mr. Warrington: Four.

Mr. Justice Sterling: I am not by any means disposed to encourage this.

Mr. Dickinson: Having regard to the order made by your Lordship, you can give me an opportunity of answering these affidavits.

Mr Justice Sterling: Have you any statement from your client as to any possible defence they can have to this action?

Mr Dickinson: I am instructed that they have raised a claim of title to these premises, which they propose to substantiate. Funds have been put together for the purpose of fighting this action.

Mr. Justice Sterling: There will be an excellent opportunity of raising a counter claim to this action: but I cannot say people are entitled to go into a man's house and take possession while he is away.

Mr Dickinson: I cannot say what my case is at present.

Mr Warrington: I must ask your Lordship to make an order in the terms of the motion.

Mr. Justice Sterling: In these circumstances I shall further restrain the defendants from further trespassing upon the plaintiff's property. If you have any case, you can make an application to discharge the order. An opportunity has been given to the defendants for the purpose of disposing of the facts stated in the plaintiff's affidavit that has not been taken advantage of. All that has been done is to change the solicitors.

Mr. Warrington: Then your Lordship will make an order restraining the defendants, their servants or agents, from being in or upon any part of the messuage and hereditaments of the plaintiff known as Shelf Hall Estate in the County of York, or committing any act of trespass thereon, or otherwise interfering with the possession of the plaintiff of the said messuage or hereditaments until the trial of the action?

Mr. Justice Sterling: Yes.

Wednesday 21st June 1893

Shelf Hall

Late in the afternoon Mr. Hainsworth, clerk to Mr. Lupton and another legal gentleman reached Shelf Hall. They met Abraham walking in the carriage drive. Mr. Hainsworth served Abraham with his copy of the notice stating the result of the court proceedings. He accepted it. A little further down the drive they met Albert. He was given his copy of the notice. Albert looked at it and enquired,

'Where is the name of the judge?'

'The proper order will come in a few days', replied Mr Hainsworth.

'Then we stop till it comes' exclaimed Albert with

determination.

The two legal men entered the hall and found Rebecca and Elizabeth sitting in the window seat of the room they called their headquarters. Elizabeth accepted her copy in silence. But not so Rebecca, who demanded to see the name of the Judge on the paper. Mr. Hainsworth explained that the proper order would come in a few days.

'I don't care I wearn't goa till I see his name theor. I wearn't go out for Cautley's lawyer', said Rebecca angrily.

Mr. Hainsworth gave up in despair and left the hall.

Late in the evening Mr. J B Jubb, solicitor, (instructed only on Monday night by Rebecca) arrived at the hall. He strongly advised them to leave the hall as soon as possible, saying there were about a hundred people at the gate anxious to see Rebecca. Rebecca accepted this advice and left the room. She was seen later walking around the grounds gathering daisies.

Figure 21. The Red Lion Inn at Bankfoot.

The family discussed how they should leave the hall. Initially the idea was to leave together in a wagonette with the bedding and tin box they had taken to the hall on the previous Monday. This, Rebecca thought, would appear an honourable defeat, but there was the possibility that they would be overwhelmed by the crowd. It was finally decided that she and Elizabeth would leave together via the back of the hall. Rebecca picked up her tin box and the bunch of daisies and held on tightly to Elizabeth's arm. The two disappeared into the darkness. They hurried towards Halifax Road in true military fashion, taking advantage of any cover afforded by trees and fences.

By the time Rebecca and Elizabeth reached the Red Lion Inn at Bankfoot, some of the other family members were already there. The atmosphere was sombre. In the eight days they had been at Shelf Hall they had become physically and emotionally exhausted. Like a retreating army Abraham, Albert and Elizabeth had lost the will to continue the fight. Rebecca tried to rekindle their enthusiasm, but due to a heavy cold she had almost lost her voice. They left the inn and went their separate ways.

Rebecca settled down in her seat on the train with her tin box and bunch of daisies. She reflected on the events of the week. She would not give in. She was confident she could muster here troops once again. She would have no sucking ducks!

Rebecca's Last Stand

Rebecca Crellin

Before the last daisy had lost its petals at Rebecca's shop in Cavendish Street Leeds, Rebecca had instructed Messrs. Johnson, solicitors, of London, to prepare an application to establish the family's title to the land at Shelf Hall. Albert was a keen trooper and no sucking duck. He was often at Rebecca's side, but Abraham and Elizabeth were not.

By mid July 1893 the case was to be heard in Chancery, but due to a legal difficulty it was postponed until after the 'Long Vacation'. The reporter from the 'Bradford Daily Argus' who had regularly reported the family's activities during the occupation of Shelf Hall, visited Rebecca at her home. The story had intrigued the 'Argus' readers and he was keen to keep the story alive by reporting any current activities. This supported the Priestley's but also helped sell newspapers.

John Edwin Priestley, Rebecca's nephew, who was the heir-at-law to the estate, returned to Bradford from his home in Middlesbrough some months later. However, like Abraham and Elizabeth, John left Rebecca and Albert to pursue their claim. They had advice from numerous solicitors in relation to the lawsuit, but made little progress in several years. A shortage of finance and competition from the Cautley barristers weighed heavily against them. But they had an ally in John Ellis. John was a member of the syndicate during the time of the litigation in 1888 he had acted on John Priestley's behalf by accepting the sod of earth which put John in possession of the land at Shelf. He acted as sole agent for the family, and with power of attorney from John Edwin Priestley.

In 1897 Nathaniel Cautley leased Shelf Hall to Samuel Oddy for seven years. Samuel invested a considerable amount of money in making the house habitable whilst converting the park into a public pleasure garden. The Bradford and Shelf tram line terminated at the entrance to Shelf Hall pleasure gardens, hundreds of people from Bradford and Halifax travelled to the gardens for a pleasant day out. During weekends and Bank holidays the park was thriving with people paying their threepence at the turnstile to gain entry to the park. Mr Oddy installed swingboats and arranged for a brass band to play to the revellers. Pork pies and soda water were sold and people were escorted around the hall.

The Priestleys soon heard about the changes at Shelf Hall and John Edwin was one of the first to arrive there on a Bank holiday, to protest to Mr Oddy. Rebecca was also a frequent visitor and on Whit Monday 1897 she too protested to Mr Oddy about his lease of what was Priestley land. As there were hundreds of people in the park at the time, she took the opportunity of taking a collection box around the park, as she had at the time of the occupation in 1893, to raise money for her legal fees.

The fight for her family's rightful inheritance of Shelf Hall estate had become an obsession with Rebecca consuming her time and money. One by one her family members had seen the futility in pursuing the case and by 1898 only John Ellis was left to support her. In January of that year she, John and a friend visited Shelf Hall pleasure gardens. The lodge-keeper was reluctant to allow her in because she often 'caused a bother' but as she said she had come to 'serve a notice' on Samuel Oddy she was allowed in. At first Mr Oddy hardly recognised Rebecca but then realised it was she. Perhaps Rebecca was showing signs of ill health. Mr Ellis handed a note to Mr Oddy:

January 28th, 1898

Samuel Oddy,
Sir;- This notice is to certify that I, John Ellis, the sole agent and manager of Shelf Hall Estate, I demand all rents and everything on the estate, both tops and bottom, belonging to the estate, must not be removed on no circumstance whatever, until they prove their tital

before the Hon. Justice Sterling, in the High Court of Justice, in London. Signed by me, John Ellis must not offer anything fore sale whatever.

No 4 Paigter Street,
Stourbridge,
Worstershire.

Mr Oddy, in astonishment, accepted the letter and referred Mr Ellis to Nathaniel Cautley. As only the tenant of the hall, Samuel was pleased to refer any correspondence of such a nature to Nathaniel Cautley. A similar letter was given to Mr Longbottom the tenant at Shelf Old Hall. The reporter commented that both letters had been 'crudely written' by Mr Ellis.

Rebecca, John Ellis and another gentleman walked around the grounds. Mr Ellis had a black leather bag over his shoulder containing the sod of earth which was dug up and given to John Priestley, at the time of his being given possession of the land. They stayed at the park for some time. Mr Oddy thought Rebecca seemed somewhat incoherent at times.

It is likely that Rebecca was ill on the day she visited the hall with John Ellis, as she died on the 29th April 1898. Her death was reported in all the local newspapers. The 'Bradford Daily Argus' reporter, who knew Rebecca well, wrote:

'There is probably no other Priestley with such pluck and determination. She was a thorough Yorkshire woman, rather rough or dialectic in speech, brusque in manner, and perhaps obstinate, but she was a good-hearted woman, who meant well, and in some respects she was gifted with natural talents of a more than average quality. She was a successful woman in the limits of her business, but so deeply imbued was she with the erroneous idea that she would some day succeed her Priestley progenitors in possession of the estate, that the purpose was quite a mania with her.'

Rebecca's widower, William Crellin married widow Sarah Ann Smallcombe on June 14th 1900 he died on June 10th 1914.

"Mad Jack" John Edwin Priestley

John, Rebecca's nephew, the heir-at-law to James Priestley's estate, was a frequent visitor to Rebecca's shop, after the family's occupation of Shelf Hall. He also visited Shelf Hall pleasure gardens to lodge his protest to Mr Oddy, the tenant at the hall, but he did not pursue his claim through the courts, he left that to aunt 'Becca. He lacked her stamina and determination, and consequently, when she died, the claim died with her. After her death in 1898 John, who liked to be called Jack, returned to Middlesbrough to Mary Jane and son Ernest. He was discharged from the Militia in 1900 and when the 'Old Queen' died in 1901, he and his family moved to Leeds in the West Riding of Yorkshire. Progress in medicine, public health, education and housing had helped to improve the living conditions and life chances of many families like John's in the early 1900's but, this was not to last, as the threat of war hung over Europe, like the Sword of Damocles. On the 4th August 1914 war was declared against Germany. This World War was to last for a further four years. The Bradford newspapers printed regular and then daily accounts of the war. The dead, injured and missing soldiers were regularly reported in the newspapers, their photographs printed under the heading 'Local Heroes in the Worlds Greatest Conflict.' Families, friends and loved ones trawled the newspapers for sight of these, often very young, 'Local Heroes'. The Bradford 'Daily Telegraph' published photographs of families and sweethearts, found on the bodies of soldiers on the battlefield, to help in their identification. Many members of John's family fought and died in this 'war to end all wars'.

After the war the Prime Minister, Lloyd George, promised the returning soldiers 'homes fit for heroes to live in and a better life for everyone'. John and Mary Jane left Leeds and moved to Bradford, hoping for a better life in his hometown. Perhaps the war had had a profound effect on John, maybe he had inherited a degree of mental illness from his mother, Catherine, who had spent her final years in a lunatic asylum, but his behaviour became a little strange. Family and friends began calling him 'Mad Jack'. John was an ill man for a year before his death, having developed bowel cancer and died in pain at his home in Pollard Street, Bradford in 1923, aged fifty-seven. John's widow, Mary Jane, married widower Arthur Wilson in 1925, Arthur died in 1930 and Mary Jane died one year later.

Politics and Emigration

Abraham Priestley

Abraham and his sister, Elizabeth, had little enthusiasm in pursuing the claim to the Shelf Hall estate and were happy to leave Rebecca and Albert to continue the fight. After Rebecca's death in 1898 and Albert's in 1903 the claim died. Abraham's nine children knew the story of their family's inheritance. The eldest son Sam had visited the hall at the time of the occupation and years later, it seems, he had booty from the hall in his cellar. These were possibly Bottomley/Cautley portraits, glass ornaments and fishing rods. Sam was a colourful character who fathered thirteen children.

Joseph, Abraham's second son had grown up listening to stories of the hardship and exploitation of the working class during the nineteenth century. The story of the worker asking his mill master for a pay increase and being told 'Aye, well 'appen we'll talk about it when trade improves' was told when mill masters like Samuel Bottomley were living in palatial property like Shelf Hall, built on land which belonged to the Priestley family.

This fuelled Joseph's interest in politics. Joseph, Arthur Tetley a fellow miner and relative of Joseph's sister, Jack Hustler and John Helliwell Squires founded the Dudley Hill and Tong Socialist Club in 1900. The club members met to socialise, drink mineral water and play card games, but their main purpose was to spread socialism. In this they were quite successful with help from the local Independent Labour Party. The Club is still active today. Kenneth, Joseph's son, was also a member of the Club. Kenneth served in the Royal Air Force during the Second World War. In 1942 Kenneth, an Aircraftman in the RAF, married Elizabeth French. Kenneth's best man was his cousin Tommy Jackson, a fellow Aircraftman and our youth of fifteen at the beginning of this story. Like his father, Kenneth was very interested in politics and in 1958 he became a Labour councillor for Bradford's Tong Ward. He remained on the Council until his death in 1970.

In the early twentieth century members of Abraham's family were disillusioned with their lives in Bradford. Joseph's ambition was to help his fellow men through socialism, while Alfred and his sister Clara wanted a better life in the United States. Alfred made his first trip to New York on the 'S.S.Lusitania' in 1909. In 1911, he with his wife of only a few weeks, Gertrude nee Bower boarded the 'S.S.Campania' for a new life in Connecticut. Clara and her children sailed on the 'S.S.Campania' in 1910 to join her husband, John Mitchell, also in Connecticut. Abraham and Emma never saw Alfred and Clara again. Their remaining grown up family settled down to life in Bradford, until war broke out in Europe.

After the war, Abraham's health began to decline. He became confused and thought his sons and daughters were his brothers and sisters. He spoke of Joseph and Grace, his parents and William and Betty, his grandparents as though they were still

Figure 22.
Kenneth Priestley's Wedding on his right is Cousin Tommy Jackson.

85

alive. He lived in the past, often talking of his childhood in Halifax and his work in the mines. Emma's anxiety increased as Abraham's general health and appearance deteriorated, and then her own health began to decline as her cancer developed. Elizabeth, their eldest daughter cared for them at home, 120 Cutler Heights Lane, Dudley Hill. Tragically January 1922 saw the death first of Abraham and only a fortnight later, Emma.

After their deaths Elizabeth decided she would join her brother and sister in America. In May 1922, she sailed in the 'S.S.Baltic' for New York. She was fifty-three and single, perhaps one of the 'surplus' women created by the loss of men in the first world war.

Following the deaths of the small band of Priestley occupiers of Shelf Hall, the memory of the claim to the estate faded.

The End of the Line

Nathaniel and Cautley

Rebecca's death in 1898 was probably a relief to Nathaniel and Cautley. Albert, Abraham and Elizabeth lacked Rebecca's determination and pluck in continuing the families' claim to Shelf Hall, so the fight died with her.

Nathaniel and Cautley continued their law practices in King's Bench Walk Temple London. Fifty-year-old Nathaniel married thirty-two-year old widow, Florence Violet Isobel Kennedy in April 1909. They lived comfortably at 89, St. Mary's Mansions, Maida Vale London, until her death, aged forty-eight in February 1924. One month later Nathaniel died. Violet did not leave a will but Nathaniel made his will thirteen days after her death, leaving his sole estate to Cautley. His solicitor and his nurse, Mary Higley witnessed this. From an estate worth £500,000 in 1893 the gross value of the estate at his death was £1087.18.0 the net value of his personal estate was £422.14.8.

Cautley had a successful law practice and a prolific literary career. He was a member of the Cornhill Magazine, a literary journal edited initially, by William Makepeace Thackeray. He wrote several articles for the magazine. In the early 1900's Cautley wrote an article "Old Haworth's Folk who knew the Brontes". This was based on an interview he had with Mrs. Tabitha Ratcliffe, the sister of the Brontes' servant, Martha Brown. He also wrote an in depth article on "Shooting Blackcock and Capercaillie in Austria". Cautley was a keen sports man and had many shooting holidays in Austria. He published three books, "The Weaving of the Shuttle", "Paul Malsis" and his book, "The Millmaster", published in 1907 was based on a mill master's family called Kildwick, and the family home called "Moorshaw". Characters in the book are said to be based on the members of his own family and the family home "Shelf Hall" His family were said to be so angry at the story and the characters portrayed that they insisted that the book be withdrawn.

Cautley died at his home at King's Bench Walk on 8th February 1926, having made his will only 3 days earlier, he was sixty-eight. He seemed particularly keen to make sure he was dead before being buried, by appointing "Dr. Aslett Baldwin or some other skilled person for the purpose of ascertaining that I am in fact dead" (for which he was to receive £50.) This was a practice more common in the Victorian era. Various bequests were made to friends and family. Family portraits, pottery, silver and furniture were left to family, friends and Pocklington church. Two Trust Funds were to be established and were to be known as "The Cautley Barkisland Trust Fund" and the "The Cautley Shelf Trust Fund". Beneficiaries of the trusts were to be the deserving poor of either parish. The gross value of Cautley Holmes estate was £4400.6.6 the net value of his personal estate was £1226.11.8.

Nathaniel and Cautley were required to change their surnames from Bottomley to Cautley to inherit from a member of their mother's family. However, the main reason for the change of name was to secure the existence of the Cautley name. This was not achieved by Nathaniel or Cautley, as neither had any legitimate children.

Two Halls Fall

Samuel Bottomley had Shelf Hall (known as New Shelf Hall) built in 1860 at a cost of £40,000. Wealthy wool manufacturers like Samuel, at the time, liked to display their wealth by having large mansions built for themselves and their family. Sadly, his wife died before it was finished. Samuel and his children lived in the house, until they left to go to boarding school. The girls married and left home. Nathaniel and Cautley went up to Oxford to read Law and remained in London. Samuel was left a lonely man in the house with only a few servants. After Samuel's death the family rarely lived in the house. At the time of the Priestley's occupation of the hall the house was unoccupied. Nathaniel had tried unsuccessfully to sell the hall at the auction in 1887. It would appear that the hall had little attraction to Nathaniel and Cautley possibly because its location was somewhat remote from society life. Perhaps its existence caused them a few problems and some bad luck. The Priestleys certainly made sure that the public knew their story and continued to be a thorn in the Cautley's side. The hall had a new tenant, Mr Samuel Oddy after the lawsuit in 1893.

Figure 23. (New) Shelf Hall with Samuel Watkinson on the front steps (By kind permission of the Halifax Evening Courier).

During his tenancy at New Shelf Hall, Samuel Oddy had developed the grounds into a public pleasure garden but, by 1905, the hall was owned by Samuel Watkinson. Sam lived at the hall until his death in 1939, when his grandson, John Watkinson, became the owner. The army requisitioned the hall in 1939 and later in the Second World War, Italian and German prisoners were detained there, the last prisoners leaving in 1948. In the following years, the hall fell into disrepair and in March 1950, Queensbury and Shelf Urban Council bought the hall for £3,000. It was decided to demolish the hall but not the coach house, stables and entrance lodge. In June 1951 the hall's massive handsome stone pillars crashed to the ground. The ground was cleared and a park created with a bowling green, tennis courts and a play area.

Shelf Old Hall, owned by James Priestley in 1747 was given to Queensbury and Shelf Urban Council by its last owner, in the hope that the site could be used for a village hall. The Old Hall was demolished in 1958, but the village hall was not built until 1975.

Life in present day Shelf village carries on oblivious to the events of the late nineteenth and early twentieth centuries. Bottomley's mill building still exists, housing a modern industry and Shelf Village Hall, built on the site of the original Shelf Hall, provides an excellent venue for community associated events. The lodge to New Shelf Hall is a comfortable family home, and on the very site of the Hall itself is a well used bowling green with a pavilion that stands where the peach house and vinery once was. Tennis courts now occupy the space that was the grand conservatory where Samuel Bottomley died. The extensive gardens are now a mini golf course. The memory of the extraordinary events of 1893 when the impassioned Priestleys seized New Shelf Hall seems now to exist only in newspaper articles and vague, anecdotal recollections.

Tempus Fugit

Grace Jackson

Grace's life had flown by since Thomas' death in 1936. She and Tommy had struggled to keep a roof over their heads through the many lean years. Tommy had served in the RAF during the Second World War, married Eileen and had two children since his teenage years at 13 Crystal Terrace, Dudley Hill, Bradford. Grace went to live with Tommy and his family at 238 Wellesley Terrace, Lumb Lane, Manningham, Bradford. Her bed, sideboard, wall clock, deal table and rocking chair were arranged in the drawing room of number 238. Grace spent most of her time in this room. She had a range, not unlike the one at Crystal Terrace on which to cook and boil her copper kettle. For the first time in her adult life she had a secure home with regular meals, coal for her fire

Figure 24. Kenneth Priestley's Wedding Guests with Thomas Jackson and Grace standing on the left, our only known photograph of Grace.

and electric lights, sharing the family bathroom and lavatory. Gone were the days of going outside to the lavatory and bathing in a tin bath in front of the fire.

Grace enjoyed the comfort and company of being part of a family again and she loved her grandchildren, Peter and Pam. She would sit in her rocking chair, in front of the fire, and chat to Peter and Pam in her broad Yorkshire dialect very much like aunt 'Becca's, who had orchestrated the Priestley's actions at Shelf Hall, and been described as a 'thorough Yorkshire woman'. Like many working women of the day, Grace always wore a pinny (pinafore). She rarely went out alone, as she was not very familiar with Manningham. Having spent most of her life in Dudley Hill, Manningham must have seemed like being at the end of the world to her.

There were few members of her family left to visit Grace as her sisters and dear brother, Alfred, had emigrated to America. She was, however, a loved grandmother and was sadly missed when she died in 1960.

The Story of my Research

I started my search into the story of the Priestley claim to Shelf Hall in 1993, at a time before the Internet was available as a source of information to family historians. As a consequence, my research has been from mainly primary sources and the newspapers of the day. My aim was always to authenticate my information.

I think it appropriate here to comment on Internet research. Some primary sources such as censuses and parish records are available to be viewed online. The census returns are indexed, which makes searching for our forbears much easier and quicker than trawling through films and fiches in libraries and archives. I visited libraries in Bradford, Leeds, Halifax and the Isle of Man to search these census sources. Now one can sit at home and search online, but as there are some mistakes in the transcribing it is essential that one consults the original source, some of which can be viewed online, but at a cost. Errors in transcription can mean that a name disappears from the index for one census, while being present even at the same address in previous and subsequent censuses. This should be taken into account when searching online indices. However, I would warn against using sources such as the Church of Latterday Saints International Genealogical Index (the IGI) as wholly accurate. The IGI, although a valuable source, must be regarded as a basis for further research and no more, although I do acknowledge the excellent achievement in its compilation. Other sources are contact websites where one may find family tree connections, which may be very valuable depending on the authenticity of information published by other subscribers.

There are, however, many gaps that I cannot fill. A family story like this one could be brushed aside as a myth or exaggeration, but there is usually an element of truth in family lore. My interest in the story was aroused when I saw a letter in the local evening newspaper from a distant relative about Shelf Hall and the

Priestley claim to it in 1893, together with confirmation from my father-in-law Thomas (Tommy) Jackson that, indeed, there had been such a claim, as he had been told by his mother, Grace.

My next source of information was local newspapers, one of which quoted Rebecca naming a James Priestley and his three sons James, Joseph and Jonathan. One newspaper had published a copy of James' will, but I also obtained a copy of it from the Borthwick Institute York. This gave me three distinct lines of James' descendents namely James, Joseph and Jonathan and by researching the parish registers I found James, Ely and William, their descendents. Probate records often have important information not always available from other sources. Interestingly the inventory that accompanied the will does not appear to be complete in that it does not include some property mentioned in the will itself. This shall remain unexplained. The inventory revealed items of furniture, including an oak bed, which I knew from the family, was still in existence in Horton, in the twentieth century. George, who possessed the bed, was easy to find, as his baptism is recorded in St. John's church register with a capital 'B' next to his name. No doubt then, that he was Rose Holroyd's bastard child.

Prior to 1837 parish registers are the main source of baptisms, burials and marriages unless one is lucky enough to own a family bible, in which these facts may be recorded. Enthusiastic ancestors may have recorded family events in notebooks, if they were literate. We have a birth recorded on the inside of the door of our longcase clock! The early parish records are notoriously difficult to read. Because the West Riding was the birthplace of most the Priestley clan it is difficult, if not impossible to be confident in proving one has the 'right' James or Joseph, being such common names. The status of the bride and groom in marriage registers reveal whether they were single, a spinster, a widow or widower, as in the case of James and his two wives Sarah and Mary. This fact gave me the information to do more research. A witness at a marriage may give the name of siblings or family friends. Occupations, if specified help pin down some ancestors. Often the Priestleys followed the same occupations from one generation to the next. Each one of these facts helped me trace or confirm several forebears. A striking observation I made from the parish registers was how many people were illiterate; very many people signed the register with a cross or other identifying mark. (Early registers were written in Latin)

Baptismal registers sometimes record only the fathers name, occupation and place of residence. The mothers name is often omitted. There were times in my research when the mothers name would have helped prove or disprove my search. Early burial registers may only give a name, date of burial, place of residence and possibly an age of the deceased. The age was often estimated. Once again, in the case of the Priestleys it was like looking for a needle in a haystack. However, my research became less difficult when the individuals' records were post 1837. Civil Registration began in 1837 when all births, marriages and deaths had to be registered, as they do today, although not compulsory until 1875. In 1801 a census of the population was recorded, but gave little information. From 1841 and every ten years since, a census return has to be collected on every member of the population, although some may have been missed. These records are available to the public to view up to the year 1901. The census gives the person's address, name, their relationship to the head of the household, age, sex, marital status, occupation, place of birth and the last column asks whether the individual is blind or deaf and dumb. Later censuses indicate senility, physical disability or mental condition. This information is invaluable, but not always accurate. The 1841 census gives less information than the later returns. The information from the birth, marriages and death registers, if dovetailed with the information on the census returns, can flesh out the bones of information on our ancestors. I was able to trace Ely Priestley and his family in Elland. I discovered Maria's absence on one census then discovered a new wife on the next census. I knew of his occupational changes from being a navvy on the canals to lock keeper, as a result of the information on the census. This also applied for James Priestley who records his occupation as 'overlooker'. This meant that he worked in the weaving of textiles but he also had some responsibility for other workers, albeit, in a disciplinary capacity.

I would not have known that Catherine was born in Ireland had it not been for the information on the census. The majority of Irish immigrants being Catholic, their religion, customs, culture and language were not tolerated by many Bradfordians; as a result they tended to live close together in certain parts of the town. The census shows areas of dense population of Irish immigrants in the town.

Joseph and Catherine's marriage was registered in 1857, so I expected to find them having set up home, with at least one child by the census of 1861, but I could not find them on the Bradford census. In 1871 their children were living with their grandmother at North Wing in Bradford. I assumed that Joseph and Catherine had died in the intervening years, had lived elsewhere after their marriage or perhaps Joseph was in prison. (One must always be prepared to find the odd skeleton in a cupboard.) I searched the prison records at West Yorkshire Archives for Wakefield and Leeds convicts but had no luck, so I checked the 1861 census for the workhouse in Bradford. What was the workhouse at this time became part of the present St. Luke's hospital. My mother -in - law, sister-in-law and myself are very familiar with this part of the hospital having trained as nurses at the hospital.

The 1861 census for the workhouse gives only initials of the paupers. This is the only census to record the paupers' initials, others record full names. But there was a female aged in her twenties, born in Ireland, with the initials C P. She had three little children M-A.P., aged 3, E.P. aged 1year and H.P. aged 1year. I felt sure this was Catherine and her children but not having their full names I had to make further checks to prove my theory. I visited Bradford Archives and searched the workhouse minute books. Fortunately they had minute books for the early 1860's and there in beautiful script was Catherine's name. Having established that this was Catherine and the girls I started looking at the 1861 census for Joseph. I found him living alone in Todmorden near some Priestley relatives and working in a local mill. I discovered this by searching his neighbours on the census. Catherine and Joseph and the girls were reunited and had further children, but on searching the 1871 census I did not find Catherine. I searched the General Register Office index for her death between 1869 and 1881. The only death I discovered was a Catherine registered in Wakefield. I discounted this one, thinking that it was highly unlikely that this would be my Catherine.

I have found over the years in my research, that somehow, in a spine tingling way, our ancestors 'will' us to find them and I felt Catherine was doing this to me, so I sent for a copy of the death certificate. A member of the Wakefield register office staff rang me a few days after receiving my request, and asked if the one he had found was the lady I was researching, as she had died in the lunatic asylum. I confirmed that it may be, thanked him for his call and received the copy of the certificate, still not sure if this was Catherine. I made an appointment at West Yorkshire Archives in Wakefield to look at the casebooks for the inmates at Wakefield Lunatic Asylum. Catherine's admission, medical examinations and death were recorded in detail. Stanley Royd Hospital, as it is now called, where Catherine lived until her death in 1874, has an excellent museum of information and artefacts. The curator is an interesting, enthusiastic gentleman.

One has to be prepared for the discovery of sad events in one's forebears' lives. I was particularly saddened when I uncovered the facts of Catherine's final years. The period I researched was one of great toil for the majority of the people in the West Riding. The story of Christmas Day that came from my husband's father became even more poignant when I read the words of Thomas Henry's memorial. Grace and Thomas were in poverty after suffering what had obviously been a 'sad life of toil and care' even when Thomas Henry was alive.

The census returns helped me plot the movements of Joseph's second wife, Ann, who was born in a pretty little hamlet in North Yorkshire. I obtained copies of marriage and death certificates of Ann and her husbands that revealed her movements. She, like so many people, left her rural way of life for a squalid urban existence in Bradford in the 1840's. Ann does not appear to have been entirely honest about her age on many official records. Our ancestors may have not known their date of birth or they liked to appear years younger than they were. If only they had known how precise we family historians like to be.

Like her brother Joseph, Rebecca Priestley eluded me for a time. She lived with her family until her marriage to Joshua Brown. She and Joshua lived in Bradford after their marriage but there were no children of theirs living with them in any of the census returns. I have not located any birth registrations or infant deaths for the couple so I assume they did not have children. Perhaps Rebecca filled this void with her fight for Shelf Hall. She had such passion, strength and determination, typical of many with the name Rebecca. On searching the 1871 census for Rebecca and Joshua I could not find them in Bradford. Once again I searched the General Register Office index for Rebecca and Joshua's deaths. I came across the death of a Joshua Brown in 1878, so I requested a copy of the death certificate. The register office staff rang to confirm they had found a Joshua Brown who had died in an accident. The coroner had reported his death and an inquest had been held to establish the cause of death. I was intrigued to find out more about this gentleman's death. Armed with my copy of the certificate I went to Bradford Central Library to look at copies of the local newspaper to see if the inquest had been reported. The inquest was reported in the newspapers and it was, indeed, Joshua Brown. Rebecca was also mentioned in the newspaper as his next of kin. This confirmed that I had found the right man. As it was quite common for our ancestors to marry several times I looked for the re-marriage of Rebecca and found that she had married a man from the Isle of Man. I felt a holiday 'coming on' on the Isle of Man. We thought it a good idea to combine a holiday or a short break with research in places that could not be reached in a day's round trip. Viewing the marvellous gardens at Kew can be combined with a visit to the National Archives, for instance.

I searched through holiday brochures and found a cosy cottage to rent at Kirk Michael on the island. I looked down the advertisement for the proprietors name and telephone number- a Mrs Crellin. I could not believe my eyes-the same surname as William, Rebecca's husband. I telephoned her to make a booking and in my effusive way I told her why we were planning a stay on the island. She said, 'hold on a minute while I look at my husbands pedigree on the wall' –pedigree, I thought, what luck, but no, no William Crellin of the dates I gave her. Serendipity, like spine tingling moments, is not uncommon in tracing family history. It turned out that the name Crellin on the Isle of Man, is like the name Brown in England or the name Priestley in Yorkshire! We searched the parish registers in the freezing cold vestry of St Michael's Church, for William's baptism and trawled the census returns for his family at the Douglas Archives Office at the top of Crellin Hill! We formed a picture of William's early life on the island and saw the site of his family's house and dye works. Only a pile of stones in the corner of a field remains of Moaneemolloch.

Rebecca wasted no time in continuing her family's claim to the Shelf Hall estate, after occupying the hall, but with no help from Abraham or Elizabeth. The 'Bradford Daily Argus' reporter appears to have had a keen interest in pursuing Rebecca's activities and reporting them, over a period of years, climaxing in her death in 1898. I spent a considerable length of time searching the filmed newspapers in Bradford Central Library uncovering this information. I wondered what had happened to Rebecca's husband, William Crellin, after her death, so I checked the trade directories at Leeds Library. Her business in Cavendish Street had been recorded in the directory, annually, before her death. New owners occupied the shop after her death, so it appeared William had moved on. As it was not uncommon for widowers to remarry I searched the General Register Office index for his marriage. William Crellin is an uncommon name, in Yorkshire, so I was quite confident when I discovered a marriage for William, in 1900. A copy of the marriage certificate confirmed my view. I was keen to have a photograph of Rebecca's shop so I contacted Leeds Archives to ask if they had any photographs of Cavendish Street taken before the demolition of the property. There were photographs, but I could not positively identify the shop from the description in the Trade Directory and the map of the day. I was happy to draw the curtain on Rebecca and pursue my next character, John Edwin.

John Edwin Priestley was the heir-at-law to the Priestley claim to the Shelf Hall Estate being in direct line from James Priestley of the 1747 will. John moved to Middlesbrough in the mid 1880's to live with a branch of the Smith/Priestley family who had originally settled there from Addingham. I have traced these families in the parish registers of Addingham Parish Church and the Middlesbrough and Addingham census returns. John married in 1888 at St. Paul's church in Linthorpe, Middlesbrough. Both he and Mary Jane could sign their names in the marriage register but John signed his middle name as Edward, he could not spell his surname correctly. The witnesses at the wedding were his aunt, Mary Priestley Smith and the church scripture reader Steeme Theulis. Steeme is recorded on the 1881 census in Middlesbrough, his children recorded as being born in Bradford, Leeds and Newcastle. This indicates that he moved around a great deal and may have met John when he lived in Bradford. It would appear that John was keen to join the army. I obtained a copy of his attestation papers from The National Archives at Kew, where these documents are held. In November 1890, John enlisted in the militia in Sunderland. He was, however, not completely honest in the details he gave on his attestation papers.

He wrongly says he was a single man and that his next of kin was his aunt Mary Ann Priestley. John was a gunner in the Yorkshire Artillery, but he was not an exemplary soldier, being absent without leave in 1897 and 1898. In 1899 he surrendered to the civil police and was tried by the civil powers. He was fined forty shillings with costs, or imprisonment, and chose to serve the sentence. In 1891 he applied to join the regular army, but he was declared "Unfit, flat footed and over age". Again he was not honest in the details he gave, having said he was a single man and giving his next of kin as his aunt Rebecca Crellin of 15 Linthorpe Mews Middlesbrough, where, to the best of my knowledge, Rebecca never lived.

I began to think that perhaps I had obtained the wrong attestation papers; perhaps these were for a different John Priestley. I compared the information on the two attestation records. His physical characteristics were the same even to the tattoo marks on his arm. He still could not spell his surname and his signature was very similar to that in the marriage register. Middlesbrough register office, very kindly, sent me a photocopy of his original signature. I do not know why he gave false information on his documents. Comments reported in the newspaper at the time of the occupation of Shelf Hall, by Rebecca, seem to suggest that the family were displeased with him.

The newspapers had reported that John had returned to Middlesbrough after his visit to Shelf Hall pleasure garden, but had he stayed there, returned to Bradford or died? There were no census returns available to view as the 1901 census was still 'in the wings'! I had found the census invaluable information in the early days of my research, although there are mistakes in some censuses. I was at a loss as to how to find John. Contrary to my principle of only using primary sources, in desperation, I wrote a précis of the Shelf Hall story, included a stamped address envelope and wrote to every 'Priestley' in Bradford and Halifax telephone directories asking for any information they might have on the family. Many people replied, some knew the family story, but none could shed any new light. I packed all my files away. I have to admit that at this point I was discouraged, and lacking the determination of my heroine Rebecca, I had a break from my research of about two years.

I took up my research again when the 1901 census became available to view, so I searched for John, Mary Jane and son Ernest. At the time of the census they were living at 17 Halton Street, Leeds. As Ernest was the only child recorded I assumed that they had no other children, or children had died before 1901, or were away from home on census night. I began the long search through the streets of Leeds for them in subsequent years, in the electoral rolls. I soon realised that this was an impossible task as Leeds was an enormous town with many John Priestleys!

I decided to search the family's whereabouts through a search for Ernest. He became the 'elusive Ernest' and has remained so. As Ernest was eleven in 1901 I assumed he would be attending school, so I made an appointment at Leeds Archives to search any existing logbooks of schools in the area. These often record children's names, addresses or items of interest about individual children. I drew a blank on this research route so I had to rethink. It was, however, possible that John and his family had remained in Leeds, returned to Middlesbrough or gone to live in Bradford, anywhere else in the country or indeed, the world. After months of deliberation I decided to search the General Register Office index for their deaths in all part of the country. I came across a John Priestley in Leeds, the right age for John at the time. I requested a copy of his death certificate only to be confronted with a similar scenario to the one I had had with Rebecca and her dead husband, Joshua. I shivered – déjà vu – the Register Office rang me to say the gentleman I was researching had died in an accident and that as the coroner had reported his death, there was no mention of a next of kin but there was his address. As I had to confirm if this was the John I was researching I requested the death certificate and went along to Leeds library to check the newspapers of the day for the result of the inquest. This John, a labourer, had been in dispute with some youths in the street, an officer in the army at home on leave at the time, had become involved in the fight, and he had struck John, who had later died as a result of his injuries. The newspaper gave no clues as to John's family other than he had a wife. I was not sure if this was my John. As the officer was to face trial at the Assizes for John's manslaughter I pursued my search for John's identity through the trial and the officer's military records, hoping that more details of the attack would be recorded. I employed a researcher to obtain the officer's military records from The National Archives but there was no additional, helpful information in them. I had hoped this route would avoid a long search through cemetery and parish registers looking for John's burial record, however it did not. I searched for John's burial at a large Leeds cemetery, his wife was interred with him and her name was not Mary Jane, so, through a long process I had eliminated John. Family history can take one up blind alleys, into brick walls and on wild goose chases but occasionally there has to be a process of elimination. At this stage in my search I decided to reflect on my methods of research and realised that I had made a most common mistake in family research. I remembered that John had always spelt his name PRIESTLY. I had been searching the index for the name spelt PRIESTLEY. I had to return to the library and check all of the indexes again.

I discovered the death of a Mary Priestley the right age for Mary Jane at the time, (with a husband named John) in Wakefield Lunatic Asylum, yet more shivers and déjà vu. John's mother, Catherine, had died in the asylum in 1874. This lady had spent time in two asylums. I had to gain permission from the local health authority to obtain a copy of her medical records. The information in these records revealed that she was not Mary Jane. I was very surprised to find a photograph of the lady in the records, taken in 1908. It was clear from the photograph that she had a goitre, (enlarged thyroid gland) which could have been the cause of her illness, a condition that was not fully understood at the time. She had also lost three children to whooping cough, a very distressing finding for me, as I have spent many years immunising children against this disease and know how simple it is to prevent.

Eventually, I came across a John Priestley in the death index in Bradford, with an age consistent with that of John's at the time. This was a 'Eureka' moment, after at least a years search. I requested a copy of the certificate and as Mary Jane, his wife, was the informant of his death I knew I had the right man. As I was still searching for Ernest I decided to check to see if Mary Jane had re-married. If she had, there was a possibility that Ernest had been a witness to her marriage. Mary had re-married but Ernest was neither a witness at the marriage nor an informant at her death.

If Ernest had survived into adulthood, which I think he had, he would have probably served in the First World War. I have searched the National Archives for his military records, but as very many records were destroyed during the Second World War I had no success. I have visited various cenotaphs to check the names of servicemen but had no success in finding Ernest. Certain family members have appeared to want to be found throughout my time in research, but Ernest remains elusive to this day. I can only assume that he died in the First World War without being recorded, his name is missing from the General Register index, I have missed it in my hasty search or he emigrated. I have checked Internet sites in America and Australia for him, without success. Perhaps he left England for some other country. I have several copies of death certificates for Ernest Priestleys from Middlesbrough, Leeds and Grimsby but none appear conclusively to be Ernest the subject of my search.

Researching the Bottomley family revealed lives of wealth and privilege in complete contrast to the Priestleys. Samuel Bottomley lived at a time in Bradford's history, when the manufacturer was king. Samuel made money and spent it. Moses and Samuel

Bottomley are well documented throughout the nineteenth century. Moses was particularly successful and played a small part in Bradford's civic and cultural life. However, Samuel appears to have been a quiet man. His obituary reported in the newspaper at the time states:

"His nature was too modest and retiring to take an active part in public life, but he nevertheless evinced a keen though quiet interest in public questions, and in public he may be best described as a Wig".

Caroline's family name was Cautley. They lived in Bishop Wilton, near York. There is a farm called "Cautley Farm" in Bishop Wilton and a small village north of Sedbergh also called Cautley. Perhaps the name Cautley originates from one or other of these roots.

Samuel died in 1883. I find it quite remarkable that Samuel did not leave a will. I have a copy of the Letters of Administration, which I obtained from the Probate Registry in York, granted to Moses Nathanial Bottomley, (Cautley) his eldest son. Sureties were Rufus and Albert Mitchell, his sons-in-law.

Effects. £20,552.00.4 Gross value)
        £ 9,513.18.8 Net value) no leaseholds

The newspapers of the day record that the land had come into the hands of the Bottomley's through a succession of trustees. For generations the Priestleys had harboured the belief that they were victims of an injustice. The Bottomleys, it seems, had little or no proof of title to the land on which the new Shelf Hall was built. There were certainly no deeds that should have existed detailing proper transactions from the possession of the Priestleys to that of the Bottomleys. Apparently, when the Priestleys disputed the title to the property in court, the only proof that could be provided was signed affidavits to say the Bottomleys had been in possession for forty years. The Bottomley's strengths were easy finance and the fact that both sons were barristers against the almost illiterate and poor Priestleys.

Early in my research into parish registers I discovered Cautley's burial in St. Michael and All Angel's Church Shelf. His brother, Nathaniel was not buried there. Once again in my research I missed the existence of census returns, I was at a loss to discover the whereabouts of the two brothers. When the 1901 census became available I found Nathaniel and Cautley living in King's Bench Walk neither of them were married. I later discovered that Nathaniel had married. At the time, I was researching Samuel Bottomley's sister, Mary Elizabeth. Her obituary was reported in the local newspapers, which included the names of those who attended her funeral. Nathaniel and his wife did not attend but sent 'floral tributes'. Therefore, I knew Nathaniel had married. I searched the General Register Office index to confirm this and a copy of the marriage certificate gave me her details. I searched the birth indexes for any children born to them but drew a blank, so I assume they had no children. I obtained a copy of Nathaniel's will from the Borthwick Institute and was surprised at the relatively small amount of money Nathaniel had left. Cautley, his brother, was the only beneficiary. Had Nathaniel had any children I feel he would have made provision for them in his will.

Cautley was a keen sportsman the fishing rods in Samuel Priestley's cellar were probably his. The Priestleys probably took some of the Cautley's possessions at the time of the occupation of the hall. The family story is that they had a bonfire with the booty. Cautley left many precious objects to his family and friends. I learned about the two trust funds set up by Cautley for the benefit of 'the deserving poor' of Shelf and Barkisland, by obtaining a copy of his will. I wonder if this was an altruistic gesture or guilt feelings on his part, for his family's method of acquiring the Priestley's land. This I will never know.

Cautley wrote several books, some of which I have read. I was lucky to find a copy of 'The Millmaster' to read, though several years' search for a copy of my own has been fruitless. Some years ago I advertised for a copy of the book, in a magazine. I had a telephone call from a lady who had bought a copy of the magazine, having never purchased the magazine before, to say she too wanted a copy. She explained the relevance of the story and the characters, in the book, which were based on the Cautley family and local characters of the day. An ancestor of hers had lived in Shelf at the time and was said to be one of the characters portrayed in the story. I felt that this was one of those spine tingling moments I had experienced before.

Visitors here in Yorkshire admire our drystone walls, but it is, perhaps, our civic buildings and ancient houses of which we should be most proud. Thomas, William and Joseph Priestley spent their working lives in digging and blasting this stone out of the ground. Like so many families at the time, they lived near each other and married local girls, often introducing sisters of their wives to their brothers and cousins. Thomas and Joseph married sisters Elizabeth and Grace Broadbent. Abraham's sister, Sarah-Ann married George Tetley, whilst Abraham married Emma, George's sister.

The census returns, over a couple of decades can reveal the rise and decline of families. This is very evident in the outcome of Elizabeth and Grace Priestley after their husbands' deaths. Elizabeth had to take in other people's washing, to make ends meet. Grace, Abraham's mother was so poor after Joseph's death that the census shows her as a 'getter up'. She had to waken those more fortunate than herself, for their work. One can only assume that, surely, a place in the workhouse would have been better than the lives Elizabeth and Grace had. But the reputation and stigma attached to being a pauper was too much to bear for most working class people. One had to be desperate to enter the doors of the workhouse. Life must have been intolerable for Catherine in the Goit Side to willingly enter the most dreaded building in any town. These several generations of Priestley families, and indeed the many Irish immigrants, played a significant role in the making of Bradford's rise and importance in the woollen, engineering and mining industries.

The General Register Office index has been invaluable to me in my recent research. I have obtained many copies of birth, death and marriage certificates mainly to identify the person I was searching and to discover their address. Armed with an address I have used the Electoral Register to trace the movements of certain people. This method is not as informative as the census, as it only records those people who registered to vote or were eligible to vote. There were no registers during the war years as voting did not occur, sadly it was this period I was researching.

I have copies of street maps of the areas and years in which the family members lived. By highlighting the streets, schools, churches, public houses, parks, places of work and civic buildings, on these maps, I felt I could walk the streets with the people I was researching. Pictures and sketches of these streets and buildings also helped me to paint a picture of their environment. Libraries, archives and newspapers often have pictures of buildings long since demolished.

Fawcett and Lupton solicitors of Leeds, who were Mr Cautley's solicitors, Lupton and Fawcett at the time of the litigation, gave us photocopies of some documents used in Chancery. Unfortunately, I was not able to trace the Priestleys' solicitor simply because they appear to have changed their solicitors often, or the records have been lost or destroyed. I have employed researchers to search the records at the National Archives for any documents relating to the litigation, but with no success. I know that there was a pedigree drawn up for the lawsuit but I have not been able to locate this. Due to the absence of a pedigree, the difficulty in reading and interpreting early parish registers and the constant repetitions of certain forenames, I have not been able to prove the connection between some generations, hence the three unconnected trees I have provided. Some of the birth dates quoted may well be baptism dates.

I am indebted to the "hacks" of the day. The reporters of all local and some national newspapers recounted the Priestleys' story, almost daily at the height of the occupation of Shelf Hall. They were very thorough in reporting even the smallest detail. The story of the litigation, occupation of Shelf Hall and the court proceedings has come from reports in these newspapers. Although the reporters of the time had an excellent command of the English language their attempts to spell out dialectal words phonetically sometimes failed to represent the correct pronunciation. I chose, however, not to change any spellings but to reproduce the text verbatim.

Anyone embarking on family research must urgently undertake two initial activities; firstly listen to members of the family and friends talk about the people, places, occupations, interests, activities, and actions of their family. Any hint of reticence may suggest a 'skeleton in the cupboard' this could mean an interesting story, shame or sadness, and must be dealt with sensitively or left well alone. Secondly, ask family and friends to look at any photographs they may have and make a note of the names, places and dates of these photographs. Photographs can be scanned electronically and returned to their owners without damage. We have few photographs of the Priestleys or anyone else in the story. The old photographs we do have were kindly given to us by a second cousin recently. Perhaps other photographs that did exist have been lost or destroyed or maybe the family were too poor to have their photographs taken. I am grateful to the reporter who described Rebecca's appearance at the time of the occupation of the hall. A photograph of her would not have revealed as much detail as his portrayal. As my research has spanned so many years, my methods of recording my findings have been a little remiss. I have some pieces of information for which I have forgotten the sources, having failed to record them. Let this be a lesson to the reader.

The two Shelf Halls have featured in the local newspapers

several times over the years, before and during their demolition. New Shelf Hall housed a variety of tenants, owners and foreign prisoners of war, during its lifetime. I was pleased to meet a ninety-year-old Italian gentleman who was an internee at the hall. He met a local Shelf girl during his stay at the hall and a romance between them, developed. They married and have four children, several grandchildren and great grandchildren. My meeting with this delightful couple was as a result of a letter I had published in a Halifax newspaper, appealing for information on my quest 'Shelf Hall'. I have found, during my years of research, that communication with the public, via the press, can be fruitful.

The large bowling green in today's Shelf Park, is the area on which the hall stood. The view from here is not unlike the view

Figure 25. Rebecca's Oak, having retained its leaves in the mild winter of 2006/7, also showing some of the original stonework in the grounds to the rear of the Hall.

the Priestleys, the bailiffs and the hundreds of sightseers saw in 1893. In 1993 we planted an oak tree in the park, that will forever be known as 'Rebecca's Oak' in memory of that week in the family's history.

The Old Shelf Hall, originally a timber framed house, later rebuilt in stone was the manor house of Shelf Hall Manor. Johannes Priestley is said to have occupied the Manor of Shelf at the time of the Dissolution of the Monasteries and it has housed many Priestley generations since. There is a well in the grounds of the hall that is still visible today. I am told Shelf inhabitants have used it in times of drought. I have not been able to locate any manorial records for the hall but antiquarians, over the years have written about its history. I am pleased to say that the Village Hall, built on its site, is an important part of the community's life.

The West Riding of Yorkshire does appear to be the geographical origin of the Priestley name. The early parish registers record the name, with its variant spellings in abundance. There are notable Priestley individuals such as J.B.Priestley, the writer and playwright, and Joseph Priestley the scientist and discoverer of oxygen. The pedigree of Joseph Priestley who was the superintendent of the Leeds and Liverpool canal until his death in 1817, suggests that his father was the son of James Priestley the will maker of 1747. If this is so, with the one exception of Rebecca, the Priestley occupiers of Shelf Hall were probably Joseph's descendants. My research has uncovered several second cousins that were unknown to my husband. One such man is coincidentally the neighbour of our good friends. Another is the daughter of the bridegroom, Kenneth Priestley, whose best man was Tommy Jackson. I had left a message on an Internet message board in 2004 and two years later the second cousin, who gave us photographs and the memorial ribbon, contacted me. All these second cousins are descended from the Abraham Priestley who was my husband's great grandfather and who took part in the occupation of Shelf Hall. His daughter Grace, my husband's paternal grandmother, visited the hall with her father.

Over the generations the family had known the story of the Priestley claim, but after the occupation of the hall and the family's failure in the lawsuit, the story had been almost forgotten. Perhaps they had accepted the failure or may, indeed have been embarrassed by it. For generations these three branches of the family had endeavoured to prove their lineage to James Priestley in and outside Chancery. Their poverty and the Cautley's wealth were, in my opinion the two main factors in the failure of the litigation.

When I first heard the few facts relating to the occupation of Shelf Hall, I was intrigued. My research has revealed amazing characters with determination, passion and obsession. These qualities were not untypical of the entrepreneurial individuals that built Bradford as the 'worsted capital of the world'. I could not allow this part of history to lie dormant so I have written this story for all those who have gone and for those who follow with Priestley roots.

Primary and Secondary Sources

Probate records for James Priestley 1747
Several other Priestley and Dixon probate records Borthwick Institute, York.
Probate records for Nathaniel and Cautley Holmes Cautley.

Baptism, Marriage and Burial records from:
St John's the Baptist Church, Halifax
St Peter's Church, Bradford.
Wibsey Holy Trinity Church.
Wibsey Slack Side Chapel
Calverley Church
St Michael and All Angels Church, Shelf
Elland St. Mary the Virgin
St Michael's Church, Kirk Michael, Isle of Man
St John the Baptist Church Coley
Pocklington Church
St Paul's Church Linthorpe Middlesbrough
St Peter's Church Addingham
Census for: 1841, 1851, 1861, 1871, 1881, 1891, 1901 In Yorkshire and the Isle of Man.

Newspapers
The Bradford Chronicle
The Bradford Daily Argus
The Bradford Daily Telegraph
The Bradford Observer
Brighouse and Rastrick Gazette
The Echo
The Halifax Evening Courier
The Halifax Guardian
The Halifax Mercury
The Leeds Mercury

The Times
The Weekly Times
The Yorkshire Post.

Bibliography

Bradford Antiquarian Vol VII *Pedigree of Priestley of Shelf and Bradford* 1933
Bradford Antiquarian Vol VII 1933 *Stott Hill Hall*
Bradford Central Library *Men of the Period* a collection of newspaper articles
William Cudworth *Rambles Round Horton.* Mountain Press 1886
Hugh Cunningham *The Invention of Childhood* BBC Books 2006
Gary Firth *Bradford and the Industrial Revolution.* Ryburn Publishing 1990
Halifax Antiquarian Society 1901-1905 *Excursion to Shelf*
Paul Jennings *The Public House in Bradford, 1770-1970.* Keele University Press
Cyril Metcalf *Shelf. Chapters on the History of a West Yorkshire Township (1086-1988)*
Local History Press. 1990
J Parker *Illustrated History of Wibsey and Low Moor*
Paul Priestley *A History of the Surname Priestley.* No date. No Publisher
The Print Unit City of Bradford Metropolitan District Council *Bradford A Centenary City* 1997
George Sheeran *Brass Castles* Ryburn Publishing Ltd 1993
Surtees Society Biography of Priestley *Yorkshire Diaries and Autobiographies Vol II*
Wibsey Slack Side Wesleyan Reform Sunday School First Centenary Booklet 1832-1932
Mechanization and Misery. The Woolcombers' Report of 1845 Ryburn Publishing 1991.

Repositories

National Archive Kew
West Yorkshire Archive Wakefield
Leeds Archive
Bradford Archive
Calderdale Archive
Teesside Archive
Worcestershire Archive
North Yorkshire County Records Office
South West Yorkshire NHS Mental Health Trust
Yorkshire Archaeological Society Leeds Family History Section
The Honourable Society of the Inner Temple.

Libraries

Leeds
Bradford
Calderdale
Douglas Isle of Man.

Register Offices

Bradford
Leeds
Middlesbrough
Wakefield
Halifax
Douglas, Isle of Man
Pocklington
Marylebone
Paddington
Dorset
Barnsley
Hartlepool
Grimsby
Southport.